Pocket
WASHINGTON, DC
TOP SIGHTS • LOCAL LIFE • MADE EASY

In This Book

QuickStart Guide

Your keys to under-standing the city – we help you decide what to do and how to do it

Need to Know
Tips for a
smooth trip

Neighborhoods
What's where

Explore Washington, DC

The best things to see and do, neighborhood by neighborhood

Top Sights
Make the most
of your visit

Local Life
The insider's city

The Best of Washington, DC

The city's highlights in handy lists to help you plan

Best Walks
See the city on foot

Washington, DC's Best...
The best experiences

Survival Guide

Tips and tricks for a seamless, hassle-free city experience

Getting Around
Travel like a local

Essential Information
Including where to stay

Our selection of the city's best places to eat, drink and experience:

◎ **Sights**

✖ **Eating**

♥ **Drinking**

✪ **Entertainment**

🔒 **Shopping**

....

These symbols give you the vital information for each listing:

📞 Telephone Numbers	👪 Family-Friendly
🕑 Opening Hours	🐾 Pet-Friendly
P Parking	🚌 Bus
🚭 Nonsmoking	⛴ Ferry
@ Internet Access	M Metro
📶 Wi-Fi Access	S Subway
🥗 Vegetarian Selection	🚋 Tram
📖 English-Language Menu	🚆 Train

....

Find each listing quickly on maps for each neighborhood:

Bar Hemingway

16 ♥ Map p233, B2

Legend has it that Hemi self, wielding a machine rate this timber-pan ered bar during showpiece is a n by Papa an town. Dress s.com; Hôtel Rit ⊙6.30pm-2a

Lonely Planet's Washington, DC

Lonely Planet Pocket Guides are designed to get you straight to the heart of the city.

Inside you'll find all the must-see sights, plus tips to make your visit to each one really memorable. We've split the city into easy-to-navigate neighborhoods and provided clear maps so you'll find your way around with ease. Our expert authors have searched out the best of the city: walks, food, nightlife and shopping, to name a few. Because you want to explore, our 'Local Life' pages will take you to some of the most exciting areas to experience the real Washington, DC.

And of course you'll find all the practical tips you need for a smooth trip: itineraries for short visits, how to get around, and how much to tip the guy who serves you a drink at the end of a long day's exploration.

It's your guarantee of a really great experience.

Our Promise

You can trust our travel information because Lonely Planet authors visit the places we write about, each and every edition. We never accept freebies for positive coverage, so you can rely on us to tell it like it is.

QuickStart Guide 7

Washington, DC
Top Sights 8

Washington, DC
Local Life 12

Washington, DC
Day Planner 14

Need to Know 16

Washington, DC
Neighborhoods 18

Explore Washington, DC 21

22 National Mall

42 White House Area & Foggy Bottom

56 Georgetown

66 Capitol Hill

82 Downtown, Penn Quarter & Logan Circle

98 Dupont Circle

112 Adams Morgan

Worth a Trip:

U Street & Shaw 110

Columbia Heights 120

Arlington National Cemetery 122

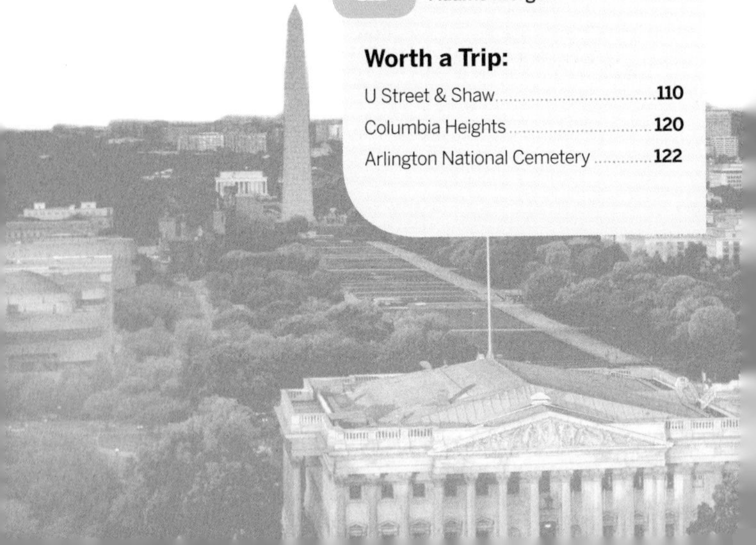

The Best of Washington, DC 125

Washington, DC's Best Walks

Iconic Washington **126**

Embassies & Mansions **128**

Washington, DC's Best ...

Eating **130**

Bars & Clubs **132**

Shopping **133**

Live Music **134**

For Free **135**

Museums & Monuments **136**

For Kids **138**

Gay & Lesbian **140**

Theater & Performing Arts **141**

Art & Architecture **142**

History & Politics **143**

Sports & Activities **144**

Survival Guide 145

Before You Go **146**

Arriving in Washington, DC **147**

Getting Around **148**

Essential Information **150**

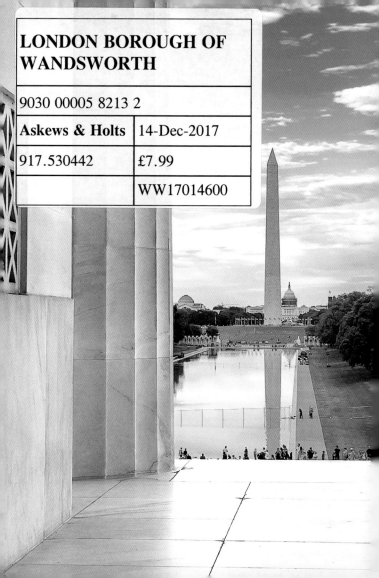

QuickStart Guide

Washington, DC Top Sights 8
Washington, DC Local Life 12
Washington, DC Day Planner 14
Need to Know 16
Washington, DC Neighborhoods 18

Welcome to Washington, DC

The USA's capital teems with iconic monuments, vast (and free) museums and the corridors of power where visionaries and demagogues roam. Seeing the White House and soaring Capitol will thrill, but it's the cobble-stoned neighborhoods, global cafes and jazzy bohemian quarters that really make you fall for DC, no matter what your politics.

Washington Monument (p28) and the Reflecting Pool (p24), viewed from the Lincoln Memorial (p24).
LUCKY-PHOTOGRAPHER/SHUTTERSTOCK ©

Washington, DC
Top Sights

IN THIS TEMPLE
AS IN THE HEARTS OF THE PEOPLE
FOR WHOM HE SAVED THE UNION
THE MEMORY OF ABRAHAM LINCOLN
IS ENSHRINED FOREVER

JEFF TURNER/500PX ©

Lincoln Memorial
(p24)

Reflect at Abe's hallowed shrine.

National Air & Space Museum
(p30)

Rockets, airplanes and spaceships galore.

Vietnam Veterans Memorial (p26)

Powerful, heartbreaking wall of names.

Washington Monument (p28)

DC's tallest, most view-tastic structure.

Capitol (p68)

Ornate halls and whispery chambers.

White House (p44)

The President's stately abode.

National Archives (p84)

Trove of historic, amazing documents.

United States Holocaust Memorial Museum (p70)

Harrowing stories of genocide.

Reynolds Center for American Art & Portraiture (p86)

Top-shelf American art.

Arlington National Cemetery (p122)

Famous gravesites and memorials aplenty.

Washington, DC Local Life

Local experiences and hidden gems to help you uncover the real city

After checking off DC's top sights, seek out the bohemian jazz quarters, curio-filled markets, sweet patisseries and arty shops that make up Washington for the locals. Count on rambling bookstores and waterfront parks making an appearance.

A Capital Day on Capitol Hill (p72)
☑ Markets
☑ Neighborhood bars

Exploring Jazzy U Street & Shaw (p110)
☑ Music venues
☑ Soul food

Strolling Genteel Georgetown (p58)

☑ Swanky antique shops ☑ Redolent bakeries

A Night Out in Dupont Circle (p100)

☑ Good-time bars ☑ Underground art

Mixing it Up in Columbia Heights (p120)

☑ Latino art and culture ☑ Hip cafes

Other great places to experience the city like a local:

National Sculpture Garden (p36)

Dumbarton Oaks Park (p62)

Grace Street Coffee (p64)

Maine Avenue Fish Market (p78)

El Sol (p94)

Seventh Hill Pizza (p79)

Dupont Circle Market (p106)

Larry's Lounge (p107)

Bul (p116)

Washington, DC
Day Planner

Day One

Dive right into the good stuff with the monuments at the National Mall's western end. The **Lincoln Memorial** (p24) is about as iconically DC as it gets. Next up is the powerful **Vietnam Veterans Memorial** (p26). Then comes the **Washington Monument** (p28), which is pretty hard to miss, being DC's tallest structure and all.

Munch sandwiches by an artsy waterfall at **Cascade Cafe** (p40). After lunch, it's time to explore the **National Museum of African American History and Culture** (p36), assuming you've procured a ticket, or the **National Gallery of Art** (p36). Pick a side: East, for modern, or West, for impressionists and other classics. Afterward, mosey across the lawn to the **National Air and Space Museum** (p30) and gape at the missiles, planes and rockets.

Hop on the Metro to Dupont Circle for dinner in one of the international restaurants. The neighborhood parties in the evening. Sip cocktails at **Bar Charley** (p107), hoist brews with locals at **Board Room** (p101) or hit one of the dance clubs.

Day Two

Do the government thing this morning. Start in the **Capitol** (p68) and tour the statue-cluttered halls. Then walk across the street and up the grand steps to the **Supreme Court** (p76); hopefully you'll get to hear a case argument. The **Library of Congress** (p76) and its 500 miles of books blow minds next door.

Continue the government theme in the White House neighborhood. Have a burger amid politicos at **Old Ebbitt Grill** (p52). Hopefully you planned ahead and booked a **White House** (p44) tour. Pop into the **Round Robin** (p53) to see if any big wigs are clinking glasses. Zip over to the **Kennedy Center** (p54) to watch the free 6pm show.

Hit Georgetown for dinner: maybe French fare at **Chez Billy Sud** (p64) or pizza at **Il Canale** (p63). After dinner, sink a pint in a friendly pub like the **Tombs** (p59). On warm nights the outdoor cafes and boating action make **Georgetown Waterfront Park** (p59) a hot spot.

Short on time?
We've arranged Washington, DC's must-sees into these day-by-day itineraries to make sure you see the very best of the city in the time you have available.

Day Three

☀ Walking around **Arlington National Cemetery** (p123) you can't help but be moved by the memorials, from the Tomb of the Unknown Soldier's dignified guards to John F Kennedy's eternal flame. The grounds spread over 624 acres and include several famous graves.

☀ Spend the afternoon downtown, where an abundance of riches await. See the Declaration of Independence at the **National Archives** (p84), and the seat where Lincoln was shot at **Ford's Theatre** (p90). The **Reynolds Center for American Art & Portraiture** (p86) hangs sublime paintings. The **Newseum** (p90) has the Unabomber's cabin. You'll have to make some hard choices about which sights to visit. When hunger strikes, try **Rasika** (p94) or **Central Michel Richard** (p93).

☾ Mosey north up 14th St NW toward Logan Circle, a bountiful food and drink zone. Buzzy **Le Diplomate** (p94) wafts a Parisian vibe, while **Churchkey** (p96) pours 550 different types of beer. Continue north and you'll come to jazzy U Street and Shaw (p110).

Day Four

☀ Start at Dupont Circle (the traffic circle) and walk northwest on Massachusetts Ave gaping at the enormous mansions along **Embassy Row** (p104). The **Phillips Collection** (p104) also spreads out in a Dupont manor; the modern paintings and sculptures provide an hour or two of groovy browsing.

☀ Adams Morgan sits just north of Dupont. It's Washington's party zone, but during the day **Meeps** (p119) and **Idle Time Books** (p119) provide plenty to do. Plus you're well situated for happy hour at **Songbyrd Record Cafe & Music House** (p118), a cool retro bar.

☾ In the evening head to Columbia Heights and see what's going on along 11th St NW. In fine weather the patio benches at **Wonderland Ballroom** (p121) fill with locals enjoying libations. And it's pretty much the same scene on up the road at wine-pouring **Room 11** (p121), beer-and-pool bar **Meridian Pint** (p121) and Italian-tinged **Maple** (p121).

Need to Know

For more information, see Survival Guide (p145)

Currency
US dollar ($)

Language
English

Visas
Generally not required for stays of up to 90 days; check www.state.gov/travel for details.

Money
ATMs widely available. Credit cards accepted at most hotels, restaurants and shops.

Cell Phones
The only foreign phones that will work in the USA are multiband GSM models. Buy prepaid SIM cards or a cheap pay-as-you-go phone locally.

Time
Eastern Standard Time (GMT/UTC minus five hours)

Plugs & Adaptors
Plugs have two vertical pins; electrical current is 120V. Overseas visitors will need an adapter and maybe a transformer.

Tipping
Expected at most places. Restaurant servers 15% to 20%. Bartenders 15% per round (minimum per drink $1). Porters $2 per bag. Housekeeping staff $2 to $5 per night. Taxi drivers 10% to 15%.

① Before You Go

Your Daily Budget

Budget: Less than $125
- ► Dorm bed: $30–55
- ► Lunchtime specials for food and happy-hour drinks: $15–30
- ► Metro day pass: $14.50

Midrange: $125–350
- ► Hotel or B&B double room: $150–275
- ► Dinner in a casual restaurant: $15–25
- ► Bicycle tour: $40

Top End: More than $350
- ► Luxury hotel double room: $400
- ► Dinner at Pineapple and Pearls: $280
- ► Washington National Opera ticket: $100–200

Useful Websites

Lonely Planet (www.lonelyplanet.com/usa/washington-dc) Destination information, hotel bookings, traveler forum and more.

Destination DC (www.washington.org) Official tourism site packed with sightseeing and event info.

Cultural Tourism DC (www.culturaltourism dc.org) Neighborhood-oriented events and tours.

Advance Planning

Three months Book your hotel, request a White House tour, try for tickets to the African American History and Culture Museum.

One month before Reserve tickets online for the National Archives, US Holocaust Memorial Museum, Ford's Theatre and Capitol tour.

Two weeks before Reserve ahead at your must-eat restaurants.

② Arriving in Washington, DC

Washington Dulles International Airport
(IAD; www.flydulles.com) is in the Virginia
suburbs, 26 miles west of DC. Ronald
Reagan Washington National Airport (DCA;
www.flyreagan.com) is 4.5 miles south of
downtown in Arlington, VA. Dulles is bigger,
but Reagan is more convenient, as it's closer
and has a Metro stop.

✈ From Ronald Reagan Washington National Airport

Metro trains (around $2.60) depart every 10
minutes or so between 5am and midnight (to
3am Friday and Saturday); they reach the city
center in 20 minutes. A taxi is $15 to $22.

✈ From Washington Dulles International Airport

The Silver Line Express bus runs every 15
to 20 minutes from Dulles to Wiehle-Reston
East Metro between 6am and 10:40pm (from
7:45am weekends). Total time to the city
center is 60 to 75 minutes, total cost around
$11. A taxi is $62 to $73.

🚃 From Union Station

All trains and many buses arrive at this huge
station near the Capitol. There's a Metro stop
inside for easy onward transport. Taxis queue
outside the main entrance.

③ Getting Around

The public-transportation system is a mix
of Metro trains and buses. Visitors will find
the Metro the most useful option. Buy a
rechargeable SmarTrip card at any Metro
station. You must use the card to enter and
exit station turnstiles.

Ⓜ Metro

DC's subway system is fast and frequent
(except during weekend track maintenance).
It operates between 5am and midnight (3am
on Friday and Saturday). Fares range from
$1.85 to $6 depending on distance traveled.
A day pass costs $14.50.

🚌 Bus

Red DC Circulator buses are useful for the
Mall, Georgetown, Adams Morgan and other
areas with limited Metro service. Fare is $1.

🚕 Taxi & Ride Share

Taxis are relatively easy to find (less so at
night), but costly. Fares are $2.16 per mile;
the meter starts at $3.25. The ride-hailing
companies Uber, Lyft and Via are used more
in the District.

🚲 Bicycle

Lots of locals cycle to get around. Capital
Bikeshare stations are everywhere; a day
pass costs $8. Bike rentals for longer rides
start at $16 per two hours.

Washington, DC Neighborhoods

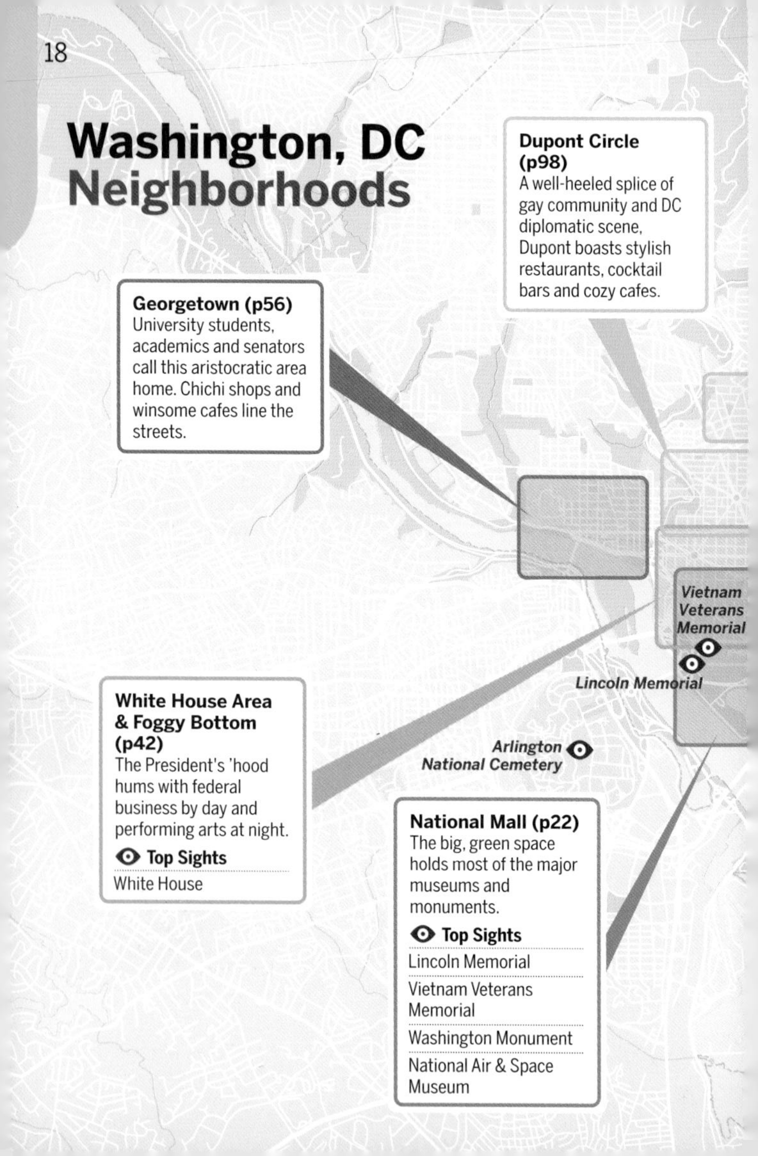

Dupont Circle (p98)
A well-heeled splice of gay community and DC diplomatic scene, Dupont boasts stylish restaurants, cocktail bars and cozy cafes.

Georgetown (p56)
University students, academics and senators call this aristocratic area home. Chichi shops and winsome cafes line the streets.

Vietnam
Veterans
Memorial
👁👁

Lincoln Memorial

White House Area & Foggy Bottom (p42)
The President's 'hood hums with federal business by day and performing arts at night.

👁 **Top Sights**

White House

Arlington 👁
National Cemetery

National Mall (p22)
The big, green space holds most of the major museums and monuments.

👁 **Top Sights**

Lincoln Memorial

Vietnam Veterans Memorial

Washington Monument

National Air & Space Museum

Adams Morgan (p112)
Browse vintage boutiques by day, dive into bars and clubs by night, eat well at romantic bistros and ethnic joints anytime.

Downtown, Penn Quarter & Logan Circle (p82)
It's a museum mecca, theater district and convention hub peppered with snazzy eateries.

👁 **Top Sights**

National Archives

Reynolds Center for American Art & Portraiture

White House

Reynolds Center for American Art & Portraiture

Washington Monument

National Archives

Capitol

US Holocaust Memorial Museum

National Air & Space Museum

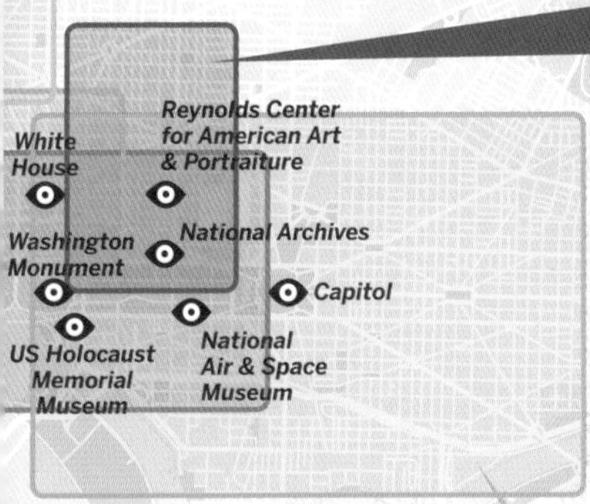

Capitol Hill (p66)
Home to the Capitol, Supreme Court and other landmarks, it's also a hub of markets, homey restaurants and cheery bars.

👁 **Top Sights**

Capitol

United States Holocaust Memorial Museum

Worth a Trip
👁 **Top Sights**
Arlington National Cemetery

Explore
Washington, DC

National Mall **22**

White House Area
& Foggy Bottom **42**

Georgetown **56**

Capitol Hill **66**

Downtown, Penn Quarter
& Logan Circle **82**

Dupont Circle **98**

Adams Morgan **112**

Worth a Trip
U Street & Shaw 110
Columbia Heights 120
Arlington National Cemetery 122

Old Guard Fife and Drum Corps in front of the National
Archives (p84)
TJ BROWN/SHUTTERSTOCK ©

Explore

National Mall

Folks often call the Mall 'America's Front Yard.' It is indeed a lawn, unfurling 2 miles of scrubby green grass from the Capitol west to the Lincoln Memorial. It's also America's great public space, where citizens come to protest their government, go for scenic runs and connect with the nation's most-cherished ideals wrought large in monuments and museums.

The Sights in a Day

Hit the west side of the Mall first and visit the monuments. It makes sense to swoop through in a counter-clockwise direction: start at the powerful **Vietnam Veterans Memorial** (p26), then walk over to the awe-inspiring **Lincoln Memorial** (p24), then on to the **Martin Luther King Jr Memorial** (p36) and **WWII Memorial** (p39). Finish at the sky-high **Washington Monument** (p28).

The Mall has so many museums, you'll need to makes some choices. Option one: delve into the intense **National Museum of African American History and Culture** (p36), provided you've prebooked your ticket; there's a soul food restaurant inside for lunch. Option two: have lunch at the **Mitsitam Native Foods Cafe** (p40), then go next door to the whopping **National Air and Space Museum** (p30). Art buffs should allot a few hours for the **National Gallery of Art** (p36), while families can immerse in the tarantula-and-diamond-stuffed **National Museum of Natural History** (p37) and pop-culture-rich **National Museum of American History** (p37).

Sup at the **Pavilion Cafe** (p40) amid whimsical sculptures. Afterwards revisit your favorite monuments illuminated at night.

◉ Top Sights

Lincoln Memorial (p24)

Vietnam Veterans Memorial (p26)

Washington Monument (p28)

National Air & Space Museum (p30)

♥ Best of Washington, DC

For Kids

National Museum of Natural History (p37)

National Air & Space Museum (p30)

National Museum of American History (p37)

Discovery Theater (p41)

Live Music

Jazz in the Garden (p41)

Getting There

Ⓜ **Metro** Smithsonian (Orange, Silver, Blue Lines) and L'Enfant Plaza (Orange, Silver, Blue, Green and Yellow Lines) for most sights; Foggy Bottom-GWU (Orange, Silver, Blue Lines) for the Lincoln and Vietnam memorials – though they're about a mile walk from the station.

🚌 **Bus** The DC Circulator National Mall bus goes around the Mall and Tidal Basin, with stops at main sights.

Top Sights
Lincoln Memorial

In a city of icons, the monument for the nation's 16th president stands out in the crowd. Maybe it's the classicism evoked by the Greek temple design, or the stony dignity of Lincoln's gaze. Whatever the lure, a visit here while looking out over the Reflecting Pool is a defining DC moment.

Map p34, A3

www.nps.gov/linc

2 Lincoln Memorial Circle NW

admission free

⊙24hr

🚌Circulator, Ⓜ Orange, Silver, Blue Lines to Foggy Bottom-GWU

The Columns

Plans for a monument to Abraham Lincoln began in 1867 – two years after his assassination – but construction didn't begin until 1914. Henry Bacon designed the memorial to resemble a Doric temple, with 36 columns to represent the 36 states in Lincoln's union.

The Statue & Words

Carvers used 28 blocks of marble to fashion the seated figure. Lincoln's face and hands are particularly realistic, since they are based on castings done when he was president. The words of his Gettysburg Address and Second Inaugural speech flank the statue on the north and south walls, along with murals depicting his principles. Look for symbolic images of freedom, liberty and unity, among others.

MLK Marker

From the get-go, the Lincoln Memorial became a symbol of the Civil Rights movement. Most famously, Martin Luther King Jr gave his 'I Have a Dream' speech here in 1963. An engraving of King's words marks the spot where he stood. It's on the landing 18 steps from the top, and is usually where everyone is gathered, snapping photos of the awesome view out over the Mall.

Reflecting Pool

Architect Henry Bacon also conceived the iconic Reflecting Pool, modeling it on the canals at Versailles and Fontainebleau. The 0.3-mile-long pond holds 6.75 million gallons of water that circulate in from the nearby Tidal Basin.

☑ Top Tips

▶ Visit the memorial at night. It's well lit and particularly atmospheric once the sun sets (plus there's less crowd jostling).

▶ For a dramatic view of the Reflecting Pool and Washington Monument, stand on Martin Luther King Jr's step and ready your camera.

▶ A small exhibit hall lies under the memorial to the south (left) side of the steps.

✕ Take a Break

Two snack kiosks flank the memorial and offer cold drinks, sandwiches and ice cream.

For coffee, beer, craft cocktails and wine, hit the casual little bar in **Hotel Hive** (☎202-849-8499; www.hotelhive.com; 2224 F St NW; Ⓜ Orange, Silver, Blue Lines to Foggy Bottom-GWU). It also houses an outpost of local chain & pizza that's open from morning until late at night. It's 0.75 miles north on 23rd St NW in the Foggy Bottom area.

Top Sights
Vietnam Veterans Memorial

A black granite 'V' cuts into the Mall, just as the war it memorializes cut into the national psyche. The monument eschews mixing conflict with glory. Instead, it quietly records the names of service personnel killed or missing in action in Vietnam, honoring those who gave their lives and explaining, in stark architectural language, the true price paid in war.

👁 Map p34, B3

www.nps.gov/vive

5 Henry Bacon Dr NW

admission free

🕑24hr

🚌Circulator, Ⓜ Orange, Silver, Blue Lines to Foggy Bottom-GWU

The Design

Maya Lin, a 21-year-old Yale architecture student, designed the memorial following a nationwide competition in 1981. The 'V' is comprised of two walls of polished granite that meet in the center at a 10ft peak, then taper to a height of 8in. The mirror-like surface lets visitors see their own reflection among the names of the dead, bringing past and present together.

Order of Names

The wall lists soldiers' names chronologically according to the date they died (and alphabetically within each day). The list starts at the monument's vertex on panel 1E on July 8, 1959. It moves day by day to the end of the eastern wall at panel 70E, then starts again at panel 70W at the western wall's end. It returns to the vertex on May 15, 1975, where the war's beginning and end meet in symbolic closure.

Mementos, Diamonds & Plus Signs

A diamond next to the name indicates 'killed, body recovered.' A plus sign indicates 'missing and unaccounted for.' There are approximately 1200 of the latter. If a soldier returns alive, a circle is inscribed around the plus sign. To date, no circles appear.

Reaction & Nearby Sculptures

In 1984 opponents of Maya Lin's design insisted that a more traditional sculpture be added to the monument. The Three Soldiers depicts three servicemen – one white, one African American and one Latino – who seem to be gazing upon the nearby sea of names. The tree-ringed Women in Vietnam Memorial, showing female soldiers aiding a fallen combatant, is also nearby.

☑ **Top Tips**

▶ Paper indices at each end of the wall let you look up individual names and get their panel location. Or you can look electronically via the Vietnam Veterans Memorial Fund (www.vvmf.org/Wall-of-Faces), which also provides photos and further info on each name.

▶ If you have questions, national park rangers are on-site from 10am to 10pm. They typically give talks on the hour.

✕ **Take a Break**

There's a snack kiosk a short distance east of the wall, at the foot of the Lincoln Memorial.

To fork into modern, locally sourced dishes head to Founding Farmers (p52); it's about a mile north via 21st St NW in the White House area.

Top Sights
Washington Monument

Rising on the Mall like an exclamation point, the 555ft obelisk embodies the awe and respect the nation felt for George Washington, the USA's first president and founding father. The monument is DC's loftiest structure, and by federal law no local building can reach above it. Alas, it is closed until spring 2019 for repairs.

◉ Map p34, D3

www.nps.gov/wamo

2 15th St NW

admission free

⏰ 9am-5pm, to 10pm Jun-Aug

🚌 Circulator, Ⓜ Orange, Silver, Blue Lines to Smithsonian

Mismatched Marble

Construction began in 1848, but a lack of funds during the Civil War grounded the monument at 156ft. By the time work began again in 1876, the quarry that had provided the original marble had dried up. Contractors had to go elsewhere for the rest of the rock. Look closely for the delineation in color where the old and new marble meet about a third of the way up (the bottom is a bit lighter).

Pyramid Topper

In December 1884 workers heaved a 3300lb marble capstone on the monument and topped it off with a 9in pyramid of cast aluminum. At the time, aluminum was rare and expensive. Before the shiny novelty went to Washington, the designers displayed the pyramid in the window of Tiffany's in New York City.

Observation Deck & Memorial Stones

Inside the monument, an elevator takes you to the sky-high observation deck that provides grand city vistas. On the way back down, the elevator slows so you can glimpse some of the 195 memorial stones that decorate the shaft's interior. Sadly, the elevator went kaput in the summer of 2016. Private funds are in hand to make renovations, but the monument won't be ready for action again until spring 2019.

Lines & Tickets

When the monument reopens, you'll need a ticket to get in. Same-day passes for a timed entrance are available at the **kiosk** (15th St, btwn Madison Dr NW & Jefferson Dr SW; ⏱8:30am-5pm) by the monument. During peak season it's a good idea to reserve tickets in advance by phone (☏877-444-6777) or online (www.recreation.gov) for a small fee.

☑ **Top Tips**

▶ Arrive 10 minutes before your ticket time, since you'll have to go through security first. The entrance area is small, and only a handful of people can enter at once.

▶ Allow an hour for your visit from start to finish. You're welcome to stay longer – no one pushes you out – but an hour is the average most people spend.

▶ Don't bring food, drinks or large backpacks. You're not allowed to take them up to the observation deck, and there are no storage lockers to put them in at the entrance.

✘ **Take a Break**

Eat a toasted sandwich while surrounded by avant-garde sculptures at the Pavilion Cafe (p40).

Head into the National Gallery of Art's Cascade Cafe (p40) for a larger spread.

Top Sights
National Air & Space Museum

The Air and Space Museum is among the Smithsonian's biggest crowd-pullers. Families flock in for the mind-blowing array of rockets, jets and other contraptions – and all of it is as rousing for adults as kids. Name the historic aircraft or spacecraft – the Wright Brothers' flyer, Lindbergh's *Spirit of St Louis*, Skylab – and it's here amid the two-floor spread of flying awesomeness.

⊙ Map p34, G4

www.airandspace.si.edu

cnr 6th St & Independence Ave SW

⊙10am-5:30pm, to 7:30pm some days

🚊 Circulator, Ⓜ Orange, Silver, Blue, Green, Yellow Lines to L'Enfant Plaza

Milestones of Flight Hall

The museum's entrance hall makes a grand impression. Walk in the Mall-side entrance and look up: Chuck Yeager's sound-barrier-breaking Bell X-1 and Charles Lindbergh's Atlantic-crossing *Spirit of St Louis* hang from the ceiling. Nuclear missiles and rockets rise up from the floor. And the moon awaits your touch (or at least a lunar rock that you're invited to lay fingers on).

1903 Wright Flyer

The Wright Brothers get their own gallery (2nd floor), and its centerpiece is the 1903 bi-plane they built and flew at Kitty Hawk, North Carolina in 1903. That's right: the world's first airplane is here. Also on display is a bicycle the brothers designed (they started with two-wheelers before moving on to flying machines) and, oddly, Orville's mandolin.

Amelia Earhart's Plane

Amelia Earhart's natty red Lockheed 5B Vega shines in the Pioneers of Flight gallery (2nd floor). She dubbed it her 'Little Red Bus' and in 1932 flew it solo across the Atlantic Ocean – a first for a woman. A few months later she flew it nonstop across the US, a 19-hour journey from Los Angeles to Newark, NJ, for another female first.

Apollo Lunar Module

It looks like it's made of tinfoil, but the Apollo Lunar Module was designed to carry astronauts to the moon. While the unit on display only flew in unmanned test missions, it's a replica of the module that Neil Armstrong and Buzz Aldrin stepped out of as the first men on the moon. It's on the 1st floor, near the Mall entrance.

☑ Top Tips

▶ Stop by the information desk and pick up a map, which shows where all the highlights are located.

▶ Download the museum's free Go Flight app, either before you arrive or on-site using the free wi-fi. It provides extra content (videos, stories etc) about popular items in the collection.

▶ Free 90-minute tours depart from the information desk daily at 10:30am and 1pm. More tours are often added if docents are available.

✖ Take a Break

McDonald's, Donato's Pizza and Boston Market are the kid-frenzied options inside the museum, all clumped together on the 1st floor's west end.

For something more offbeat, try the Mitsitam Native Foods Cafe (p40) in the American Indian Museum next door.

Skylab Orbital Workshop

Skylab was America's first space station, launched in 1973. The orbital workshop was its largest component, and was where the astronauts lived. Crews of three stayed aboard for up to three months. Walk through to see the shower, exercise bicycle and other cramped quarters. It definitely isn't a lifestyle for claustrophobes. It's in the Space Race gallery (1st floor).

How Things Fly Gallery

On the 1st floor near the information desk, How Things Fly whooshes with interactive gadgets for young ones. Kids can find out their weight on the moon, see a wind tunnel in action and make awesome paper airplanes.

Flight Simulators

Thrill-seekers should head to the Flight Simulator Zone on the 1st floor. It offers two experiences. One is a badass aerial-combat trip, where participants control the action. The other is a more passive 'ride' aboard an F-18 or cosmic coaster. The simulators cost $8 to $10 per person.

Imax Theater & Planetarium

The Lockheed Martin Imax Theater screens a rotating list of films throughout the day. Shows at the Albert Einstein Planetarium send viewers hurtling through space on tours of the universe. Buy your tickets as soon as you arrive, or on the museum website before you visit. Tickets cost $9; there's a surcharge for online orders.

Museum Annex

Only a fraction of the museum's planes and spacecraft fit into the building on the Mall. The leftovers fill two enormous hangars at the Steven F Udvar-Hazy Center near Dulles Airport. Highlights include the *Enola Gay* (the B-29 that dropped the atomic bomb on Hiroshima) and Space Shuttle *Discovery*. The annex is 2.5 miles (about a $12 taxi ride) from Dulles.

Understand

Who was James Smithson?

The Big Gift

James Smithson was a British scientist who never set foot in the USA, let alone Washington, DC. Yet he died in 1829 with a provision in his will to found 'at Washington, under the name of the Smithsonian Institution, an establishment for the increase and diffusion of knowledge.' Actually, that was the backup plan. The money first went to his nephew Henry, but Henry died a few years after Smithson, without heirs. So the 'institution' clause kicked in, and $508,318 arrived in Washington for the task.

The US government promptly ignored the amazing gift. Various senators grumbled it was undignified for America to accept such presents, particularly from an unknown foreigner. Anti-British sentiment informed some of this debate: the 1814 British torching of Washington remained fresh in many American minds. Finally though, Congress accepted the money and began constructing the Smithsonian Institution in 1846.

Mysterious Motive

So who was Smithson? A mineralogist by trade and shrewd investor by evidence (his donation was a fortune for its time), Smithson was well educated and wealthy by any measure. But his motivations for bequeathing so much money to the USA, as opposed to his native Britain, remain a mystery. Some say he was an anti-monarchist who took a particular shine to the American Republic. He may have just loved learning.

Smithson was 64 years old when he died in Genoa, Italy, and was buried there, until Alexander Graham Bell – in his role as Smithsonian regent – went to fetch the Englishman's remains and bring them to Washington in 1904. Today Smithson is entombed in the Smithsonian Castle on the Mall.

The Smithsonian Today

Smithson's gift morphed into a vast vault of treasures. The Smithsonian holds approximately 156 million artworks, scientific specimens, artifacts and other objects, of which less than 2% are on display at any given time. The collection sprawls across 19 museums – 10 on the Mall, seven others around DC and two in New York City. The Smithsonian also operates the National Zoo. There is no entry fee for any of the venues.

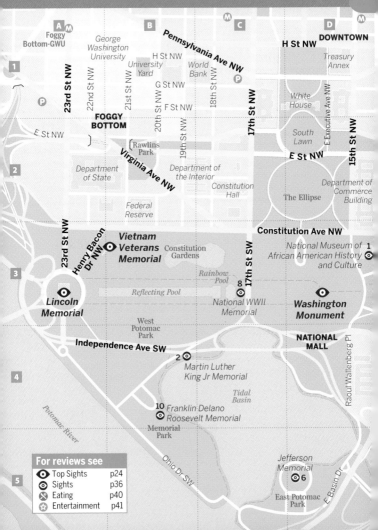

A
B
C
D

George Washington University

Pennsylvania Ave NW

H St NW

DOWNTOWN

H St NW

Treasury Annex

University Yard

World Bank

White House

23rd St NW

22nd St NW

21st St NW

G St NW

F St NW

18th St NW

17th St NW

E Executive Ave NW

FOGGY BOTTOM

20th St NW

19th St NW

South Lawn

15th St NW

E St NW

E St NW

〔Rawlins Park〕

Virginia Ave NW

Department of State

Department of the Interior

The Ellipse

Department of Commerce Building

Federal Reserve

Constitution Hall

Constitution Ave NW

23rd St NW

Henry Bacon Dr NW

Vietnam Veterans Memorial Ⓞ

Constitution Gardens

National Museum of African American History and Culture Ⓞ **1**

17th St SW

Rainbow Pool

Reflecting Pool

8 Ⓞ

Ⓞ

Lincoln Memorial Ⓞ

National WWII Memorial

Washington Monument

West Potomac Park

Independence Ave SW

NATIONAL MALL

2 Ⓞ

Raoul Wallenberg Pl

Martin Luther King Jr Memorial

Tidal Basin

10 Franklin Delano Ⓞ Roosevelt Memorial

Potomac River

Memorial Park

Ohio Dr SW

Jefferson Memorial

Ⓞ **6**

East Potomac Park

E Basin Dr

For reviews see	
Ⓞ Top Sights	p24
Ⓞ Sights	p36
Ⓧ Eating	p40
☆ Entertainment	p41

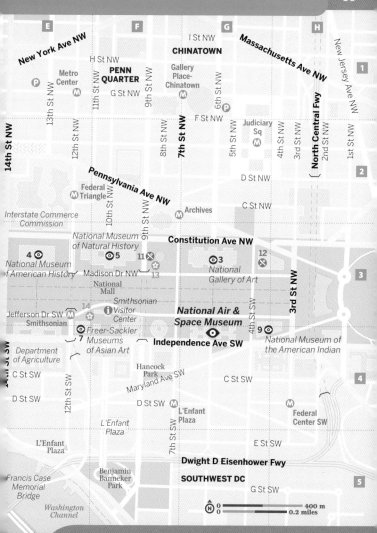

Sights

National Museum of African American History & Culture
MUSEUM

 1 Map p34, D3

Opened in 2016, the Smithsonian's newest museum covers the diverse African American experience and how it helped shape the nation. The collection includes everything from Harriet Tubman's hymnal to Louis Armstrong's trumpet. The museum is so wildly popular you need a timed entry pass to get in. Your best bet to obtain one is via the same-day online release, when tickets are made available at 6:30am on the museum's website. Be ready, because they're snapped up within

minutes. (📞844-750-3012; www.nmaahc.si.edu; 1400 Constitution Ave NW; admission free; ⏱10am-5:30pm; 🚌Circulator, Ⓜ️Orange, Silver, Blue Lines to Smithsonian or Federal Triangle)

Martin Luther King Jr Memorial
MONUMENT

2 Map p34, B4

Opened in 2011, this is the Mall's newest memorial and the first one to honor an African American. Sculptor Lei Yixin carved the piece. Besides Dr King's striking, 30ft-tall image, known as the Stone of Hope, there are two blocks of granite behind him that represent the Mountain of Despair. A wall inscribed with King's moving quotes about democracy, justice and peace flanks the piece. It sits in a lovely spot on the banks of the Tidal Basin. (www.nps.gov/mlkm; 1850 W Basin Dr SW; admission free; ⏱24hr; 🚌Circulator, Ⓜ️Orange, Silver, Blue Lines to Smithsonian)

National Gallery of Art
MUSEUM

3 Map p34, G3

The staggering collection spans the Middle Ages to the present. The neoclassical west building showcases European art through the early 1900s; highlights include the Western Hemisphere's only da Vinci painting and a slew of impressionist and postimpressionist works. The IM Pei–designed east building displays modern art, with works by Picasso, Matisse, Pollock and a massive Calder mobile over the entrance lobby. Recently renovated

---

⭕ Local Life

National Sculpture Garden

The 6-acre **National Sculpture Garden** (cnr Constitution Ave NW & 7th St NW; admission free; ⏱10am-6pm Mon-Thu & Sat, 10am-8:30pm Fri, 11am-6pm Sun; 🚌Circulator, Ⓜ️Green, Yellow Lines to Archives) is studded with whimsical sculptures such as Roy Lichtenstein's *House* and Louise Bourgeois' leggy *Spider*. They are scattered around a fountain – a great place to dip your feet in summer and join the locals who are hanging out. From mid-November to mid-March the fountain becomes a festive ice rink.

ANTON_IVANOV/SHUTTERSTOCK ©

National Gallery of Art interior

and expanded, this new wing really dazzles. A trippy underground walkway connects the two buildings. (☎202-737-4215; www.nga.gov; Constitution Ave NW, btwn 3rd & 7th Sts; admission free; ☺10am-5pm Mon-Sat, 11am-6pm Sun; ☐Circulator, Ⓜ Green, Yellow Lines to Archives)

National Museum of American History
MUSEUM

4 ◉ Map p34, E3

The museum collects all kinds of artifacts of the American experience. The centerpiece is the flag that flew over Fort McHenry in Baltimore during the War of 1812 – the same flag that inspired Francis Scott Key to pen 'The Star-Spangled Banner'. Other highlights include Julia Child's kitchen, Dorothy's ruby slippers and a piece of Plymouth Rock. (☎202-663-1000; www.americanhistory.si.edu; cnr 14th St & Constitution Ave NW; admission free; ☺10am-5:30pm, to 7:30pm some days; ☐Circulator, Ⓜ Orange, Silver, Blue Lines to Smithsonian or Federal Triangle)

National Museum of Natural History
MUSEUM

5 ◉ Map p34, F3

Smithsonian museums don't get more popular than this one, so crowds are pretty much guaranteed. Wave to Henry, the elephant who guards the rotunda, then zip to the 2nd floor's Hope Diamond. The 45.52-carat bauble has cursed its owners, including Marie

Understand

Mall of Justice

The Mall has long provided a forum for people seeking to make their grievances heard by the government. Suffragists, veterans, peaceniks, civil-rights activists, sharecroppers and million-mom marchers, among many other groups, have all staged political rallies on the Mall over the years.

Key Events in History

Bonus Army (1932) WWI veterans, left unemployed by the Great Depression, petitioned the government for an early payment of promised bonuses for their wartime service. As many as 10,000 veterans settled in for an extended protest, pitching tents on the Mall and the Capitol lawn.

'I Have a Dream' (1963) At the zenith of the Civil Rights movement, Reverend Martin Luther King's stirring speech, delivered from the steps of the Lincoln Memorial to 200,000 supporters, remains a high point in the struggle for racial equality.

Anti-War Protests (1971) In April 1971 an estimated 500,000 Vietnam veterans and students gathered on the Mall to oppose continued hostilities. Several thousand arrests were made.

AIDS Memorial Quilt (1996) Gay and lesbian activists drew more than 300,000 supporters in a show of solidarity for equal rights under the law and to display the ever-growing AIDS quilt, which covered the entire eastern flank of the Mall from the Capitol to the Washington Monument.

Million-Mom March (2000) A half-million people convened on the Mall on Mother's Day to draw attention to handgun violence and to demand that Congress pass stricter gun-ownership laws.

Bring Them Home Now Tour (2005) Led by families who lost loved ones in the war, this gathering of over 100,000 protesters demanded the withdrawal of American soldiers from Iraq.

Women's March (2017) The day after President Donald Trump's inauguration, some 500,000 people gathered on the Mall to advocate for women's rights and other issues. Concurrent marches were held in cities around the globe.

Antoinette, or so the story goes. The beloved dinosaur hall is under renovation until 2019, but the giant squid and tarantula feedings fill in the thrills at this kid-packed venue. (☎202-663-1000; www.naturalhistory.si.edu; cnr 10th St & Constitution Ave NW; admission free; ⏱10am-5:30pm, to 7:30pm some days; 🚌Circulator, Ⓜ Orange, Silver, Blue Lines to Smithsonian or Federal Triangle)

Jefferson Memorial MONUMENT

6 ◎ Map p34, D5

Set on the south bank of the Tidal Basin amid the cherry trees, this memorial honors the third US president, political philosopher, drafter of the Declaration of Independence and founder of the University of Virginia. Inside is a 19ft bronze likeness, and excerpts from Jefferson's writings are etched into the walls. (www.nps.gov/thje; 900 Ohio Dr SW; admission free; ⏱24hr; 🚌Circulator, Ⓜ Orange, Silver, Blue Lines to Smithsonian)

Freer-Sackler Museums of Asian Art MUSEUM

7 ◎ Map p34, E4

Japanese silk scrolls, rare Islamic manuscripts and Chinese jades spread through cool, quiet galleries. The Freer and Sackler are actually separate venues, connected by an underground tunnel. The Sackler focuses more on changing exhibits, while the Freer, rather incongruously, also houses works by American painter James Whistler. Don't miss the blue-and-gold,

ceramics-crammed Peacock Room. (☎202-633-1000; www.asia.si.edu; cnr Independence Ave & 12th St SW; admission free; ⏱10am-5:30pm; 🚌Circulator, Ⓜ Orange, Silver, Blue Lines to Smithsonian)

National WWII Memorial MONUMENT

8 ◎ Map p34, C3

Dedicated in 2004, the WWII memorial honors the 400,000 Americans who died in the conflict, along with the 16 million US soldiers who served between 1941 and 1945. The plaza's dual arches symbolize victory in the Atlantic and Pacific theaters. The 56 surrounding pillars represent each US state and territory. You'll often see groups of veterans paying their respects here. (www.nps.gov/wwii; 17th St; admission free; ⏱24hr; 🚌Circulator, Ⓜ Orange, Silver, Blue Lines to Smithsonian)

National Museum of the American Indian MUSEUM

9 ◎ Map p34, G4

Ensconced in honey-colored, undulating limestone, this museum makes a striking architectural impression. Inside it offers cultural artifacts, costumes, video and audio recordings. The 'Our Universes' gallery about Native American beliefs and creation stories is intriguing and a good place to start. (☎202-663-1000; www.nmai.si.edu; cnr 4th St & Independence Ave SW; admission free; ⏱10am-5:30pm; 🚌Circulator, Ⓜ Orange, Silver, Blue, Green, Yellow Lines to L'Enfant Plaza)

Top Tip

Bring a Picnic

Aside from a couple of notable museum cafes and scattered snack vendors, it's a food desert on the Mall. It's wise to bring your own nibbles. One strategy: hit Eastern Market first to assemble a picnic for later in the day. It's a short hop east on the Metro's Blue, Orange and Silver Lines in the Capitol Hill neighborhood.

Franklin Delano Roosevelt Memorial

MONUMENT

10 ◉ Map p34, B4

The 7.5-acre memorial pays tribute to the longest-serving president in US history. Visitors are taken through four red-granite 'rooms' that narrate FDR's time in office, from the Depression to the New Deal to WWII. The story is told through statuary and inscriptions, punctuated with fountains and peaceful alcoves. It's especially pretty at night, when the marble shimmers in the glossy stillness of the Tidal Basin. The irony is, FDR didn't want a grand memorial. Instead, he requested a modest **stone slab** (cnr 9th St & Pennsylvania Ave NW; Ⓜ Archives) by the National Archives building. (www.nps.gov/frde; 400 W Basin Dr SW; admission free; ⏱ 24hr; 🚌 Circulator, Ⓜ Orange, Silver, Blue Lines to Smithsonian)

Eating

Mitsitam Native Foods Cafe

NATIVE AMERICAN **$$**

Certainly the most unique food on the Mall, Mitsitam (see 9 ◉ Map p34; G4) introduces visitors to the Native American cuisine of five different regions, including the Northwest coast (such as cedar-planked wild salmon), Great Plains (buffalo chili) and northern woodlands (maple-brined turkey and wild rice). Menus rotate seasonally. It's a cafeteria-style set-up. (www.mitsitam cafe.com; cnr 4th St & Independence Ave SW, National Museum of the American Indian; mains $12-22; ⏱ 11am-5pm, reduced hours in winter; 🚌 Circulator, Ⓜ Orange, Silver, Blue, Green, Yellow Lines to L'Enfant Plaza)

Pavilion Cafe

CAFE **$**

11 ✖ Map p34, F3

Set amid the rambling sylvan serenity of the National Sculpture Garden, this pizza and panini place bustles throughout the seasons. Eat in the glass-walled interior or at the umbrella-shaded outdoor tables. The cafe makes a sweet pit stop for a French pastry and glass of wine or beer. (📞 202-289-3361; www. pavilioncafe.com; cnr Constitution Ave & 7th St NW; mains $9-12; ⏱ 10am-6pm Mon-Thu & Sat, to 8:30pm Fri, 11am-6pm Sun; 🚌 Circulator, Ⓜ Green, Yellow Lines to Archives)

Cascade Cafe

CAFE **$**

12 ✖ Map p34, G3

Located at the juncture of the National Gallery's two wings, the

Mitsitam Native Foods Cafe

Cascade offers views of just that: a shimmering, artificial waterfall. The cafeteria-style eatery is divided into different stations where you pick up a tray and choose from pizza, pasta, sandwiches, barbecue and salads. The adjoining espresso bar scoops 19 flavors of gelato. (☎202-842-6679; National Gallery of Art, East Bldg; mains $7-14; ⊙11am-3pm Mon-Sat, to 4pm Sun; 🚌Circulator, Ⓜ Green, Yellow Lines to Archives)

Entertainment

Jazz in the Garden LIVE MUSIC

 13 ⭐ Map p34, F3

Lots of locals show up for these free outdoor jazz, blues and world-music concerts at the National Sculpture Garden. Bring a blanket and picnic fare, and supplement with beverages from the Pavilion Cafe. (www.nga.gov/jazz; cnr Constitution Ave & 7th St NW; admission free; ⊙5-8:30pm Fri late May–late Aug; 🚌Circulator, Ⓜ Green, Yellow Lines to Archives)

Discovery Theater THEATER

14 ⭐ Map p34, E3

In the basement of the Ripley Center, Discovery stages delightful puppet shows and other productions for children. (☎202-633-8700; www.discovery theater.org; 1100 Jefferson Dr SW; tickets $6-12; 🚌Circulator, Ⓜ Orange, Silver, Blue Lines to Smithsonian)

Explore

White House Area & Foggy Bottom

The president lives at the center of the 'hood. The State Department, World Bank and other institutions hover nearby in Foggy Bottom. It's mostly a business district by day, and not terribly active by night, with the exception of the Kennedy Center for performing arts. Fine dining restaurants and Manhattan-stirring politician bars are scattered throughout.

The Sights in a Day

☼ Begin with the big one: the **White House** (p44). Even if you don't get in for a public tour, you can catch a glimpse of the house across the North or South Lawn and check out presidential exhibits in the visitor center. Mosey around the monument-studded **Ellipse** (p50).

☼ **Old Ebbitt Grill** (p52) has been around forever, serving burgers, seafood and booze; keep an eye out for political big wigs during lunch. See what crafty exhibitions are on at the **Renwick Gallery** (p50) and **Textile Museum** (p50). Go for drinks at **Round Robin** (p53) or **Off the Record** (p53), a couple of age-old bars frequented by politicos who like their martinis and Scotch.

☾ Have at dinner at rustic-cool **Founding Farmers** (p52) or classy French **Marcel's** (p52). Early birds can catch the free daily 6pm performance at the **Kennedy Center** (p54); otherwise get tickets for the opera or symphony later in the evening. Incidentally, the big building next door to the Kennedy is the **Watergate Complex** (p50; pictured left). Rock and rollers can see what's on at the **Hamilton** (p54).

👁 Top Sight
White House (p44)

♥ Best of Washington, DC

History & Politics
Round Robin (p53)

Off the Record (p53)

Old Ebbitt Grill (p52)

Watergate Complex (p50)

Theater & Performing Arts
Kennedy Center (p54)

Shopping
White House Gifts (p54)

Live Music
Hamilton (p54)

Getting There

Ⓜ **Metro** The Orange, Silver and Blue Lines run in tandem here. Get off at Federal Triangle or McPherson Sq for the White House; Farragut West for the Renwick and other museums; and Foggy Bottom-GWU for the university and Kennedy Center.

Top Sights
White House

The White House is a home as well as a symbol. It stuns visitors with its sense of pomp and circumstance, yet it also charms with little traces left behind by those who have lived here before, which includes every US president since John Adams. Icon of the American presidency? Yeah. But it's also someone's home.

👁 Map p48, F3

www.whitehouse.gov

1600 Pennsylvania Ave NW

🕐 tours 7:30-11:30am Tue-Thu, to 1:30pm Fri & Sat

Ⓜ Orange, Silver, Blue Lines to Federal Triangle or McPherson Sq

The Design

George Washington picked the site for the White House in 1791. Pierre L'Enfant was the initial architect, but he was fired for insubordination. Washington held a national competition to find a new designer. Irish-born architect James Hoban won. His idea was to make the building simple and conservative in keeping with the new country's principles. He modeled the neoclassical-style manor on Leinster House, a mid-18th-century duke's villa in Dublin that still stands and is now used by Ireland's Parliament.

The Color

The 'President's House' was built between 1792 and 1800. Legend has it that after the British burned the building in the War of 1812, the house was restored and painted white to cover the smoke marks, and people began to call it the White House. That's not true – it had been white almost from the get-go – but it makes a nice story. Hoban, incidentally, was hired to supervise the rebuilding. It was a big job, as all that remained were the exterior walls and interior brickwork.

The Residence

The White House has 132 rooms and 35 bathrooms. This includes 412 doors, 147 windows, 28 fireplaces, eight staircases and three elevators. The Residence is in the middle, flanked by the East and West Wings. The Residence has three main levels: the Ground Floor, State Floor and Second Floor. The Ground and State Floors have rooms used for official entertaining and ceremonial functions. The Second Floor holds the private living quarters of the president and family.

East & West Wings

The East and West Wings are on either side of the Residence. In general, the West Wing is the

---

☑ Top Tips

▶ Bring your smartphone or compact camera. Photos are permitted on the tours using these devices, though no video, flash photography or lenses longer than 3in are allowed.

▶ Do not bring backpacks, purses, food or bottled beverages. They are not permitted on the tour, and there are no lockers on site.

▶ Use the bathroom before arriving, as there are no public facilities at the White House. The closest restroom is at the Ellipse visitor pavilion.

▶ It's fine to ask the Secret Service members standing guard in each room questions about the house's history and architecture.

✗ Take a Break

Go where the political players go: Old Ebbitt Grill (p52) for burgers, oysters and a nice cabernet sauvignon; or Round Robin (p53) for a mint julep or single-malt Scotch.

business side, and the East Wing is the social side. So the Situation Room – a 5000-sq-ft complex staffed 24/7 to monitor national and world intelligence information – is in the West Wing. The Cabinet Room is there too, with its huge mahogany table around which the cabinet secretaries sit to discuss business with the president. The East Wing – where the public tours begin – holds the first lady's office, the social secretary's office, and the Graphics and Calligraphy Office (though you won't see any of these).

Personal Touches

Presidents have customized the property over time. Franklin Roosevelt added a pool; Truman gutted the whole place (and simply discarded many of its historical features – today's rooms are replicas); Jacqueline Kennedy brought back antique furnishings and historic details; Nixon added a bowling alley; Carter installed solar roof panels, which Reagan then removed; Clinton added a jogging track; and George W Bush included a T-ball field.

Tours

Tours are free, but they have to be arranged in advance. Americans must apply via one of their state's members of Congress, and non-Americans must apply through their country's embassy in DC. Applications are taken from 21 days to three months in advance; the earlier you request during this time frame the better. Don't take it personally if you don't get accepted. Capacity is limited, and often official events take precedence over public tours. If you do get in, the self-guided walk-through takes about 30 minutes.

Visitor Center

The **White House Visitor Center** (☏20 2-208-1631; www.nps.gov/whho; 1450 Pennsylvania Ave NW; admission free; ⏰7:30am-4pm; Ⓜ Orange, Silver, Blue Lines to Federal Triangle) is your backup plan. Browse artifacts such as Roosevelt's desk for his fireside chats and Lincoln's cabinet chair. See the chocolate molds that White House pastry chefs use. Multimedia exhibits give a 360-degree view into the White House's rooms. It's obviously not the same as seeing the real deal first-hand, but the center does do its job very well, giving a comprehensive history sprinkled with great anecdotes on presidential spouses, kids, pets and dinner preferences. The gift shop is excellent.

Best Photo Opportunities

Want to snap a selfie with a White House backdrop? You have two options. First head to Pennsylvania Ave, past the peace activists who are always there, for photos across the North Lawn. This view shows the triangular north portico and main driveway. Then walk to E St NW for pictures with a South Lawn background. The view here focuses on the rounded south portico and distant flowery gardens. Alas, there's a security barrier between you and the White House fence, so you won't be getting any unfettered close-ups.

The Blue Room in the White House

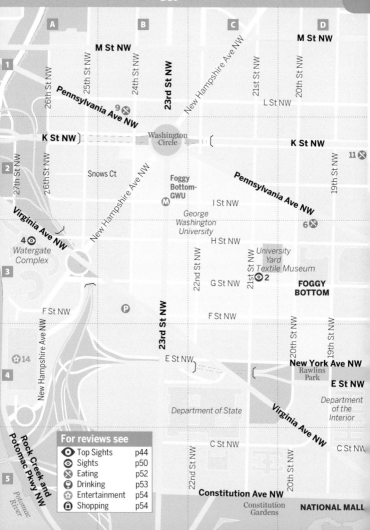

M St NW

A   B   C   D

M St NW

1

25th St NW
24th St NW
23rd St NW
21st St NW
20th St NW

Pennsylvania Ave NW

26th St NW

L St NW

9 ⊗

K St NW]

Washington Circle

[K St NW

11 ⊗

2

27th St NW
26th St NW
19th St NW

Snows Ct

New Hampshire Ave NW

Foggy Bottom-GWU
Ⓜ

Pennsylvania Ave NW

I St NW

6 ⊗

Virginia Ave NW

George Washington University

H St NW

University Yard Textile Museum
◎ 2

4 ◎

Watergate Complex

3

22nd St NW
21st St NW

G St NW

FOGGY BOTTOM

F St NW

Ⓟ

F St NW

20th St NW
19th St NW

23rd St NW

New Hampshire Ave NW

E St NW

New York Ave NW

⊕ 14

[

]

Rawlins Park

E St NW

4

Department of the Interior

Department of State

Virginia Ave NW

C St NW

C St NW

Rock Creek and Potomac Pkwy NW

22nd St NW
20th St NW

For reviews see	
◉ Top Sights	p44
◎ Sights	p50
⊗ Eating	p52
⊜ Drinking	p53
⊕ Entertainment	p54
⚿ Shopping	p54

5

Potomac River

Constitution Ave NW

Constitution Gardens

NATIONAL MALL

Connecticut Ave NW

18th St NW

17th St NW

16th St NW

15th St NW

Vermont Ave NW

Thomas Circle

M St NW

13th St NW

L St NW

0   400 m
0   0.2 miles

Ⓜ Farragut North

K St NW

Farragut Sq

McPherson Sq

Franklin Sq

Ⓜ Farragut West

Connecticut Ave NW

I St NW

Vermont Ave NW

15th St NW

Ⓜ McPherson Sq

Zei Al NW

H St NW

12 Ⓞ

✕ 7

New York Ave NW

Ⓧ 10

Lafayette Sq

Treasury Annex

DOWNTOWN

1 Renwick
Ⓞ Gallery

Pennsylvania Ave NW

Ⓟ

G St NW

🔒16

Ⓟ

G St NW

13th St NW

Metro Center

Ⓜ

White House
Ⓞ

🔒17

15th St NW

14th St NW

Ⓧ 8

15 ☆

F St NW

Ⓜ Metro Center

17th St NW

F St NW

18th St NW

Old Executive Office Building

Department of the Treasury

F St NW

12th St NW

13

South Lawn

E St NW

Pennsylvania Ave NW

Pennsylvania Ave NW

D St NW

5 Ⓞ

Ⓞ3

Ellipse

Department of Commerce Building

Ⓜ Federal Triangle

Daughters of the American Revolution

Constitution Ave NW

National Mall

Sights

Renwick Gallery MUSEUM

1 Map p48, E3

Part of the Smithsonian diaspora, the Renwick Gallery is set in a stately 1859 mansion and exhibits a playful collection of contemporary American crafts and decorative-art pieces. (☏202-633-7970; http://renwick.americanart.si.edu; 1661 Pennsylvania Ave NW; admission free; ⏱10am-5:30pm; Ⓜ Orange, Silver, Blue Lines to Farragut West)

Textile Museum MUSEUM

2 Map p48, C3

This gem is the country's only textile museum. Galleries spread over two floors hold exquisite fabrics and carpets. Exhibits revolve around a theme, say Asian textiles depicting dragons or Kuba cloth from the Democratic Republic of Congo, and rotate a few times a year. Bonus: the museum shares space with George Washington University's Washingtonia trove of historic maps, drawings and ephemera. (☏202-994-5200; www.museum.gwu.edu; 701 21st St NW; suggested donation $8; ⏱11am-5pm Mon & Fri, 11am-7pm Wed & Thu, 10am-5pm Sat, 1-5pm Sun; Ⓜ Orange, Silver, Blue Lines to Foggy Bottom-GWU)

Ellipse PARK

3 Map p48, F5

The expansive, oval-shaped park on the White House's south side is known as the Ellipse. It's studded with a random collection of monuments, such as the Zero Milestone (the marker for highway distances all across the country). It also hosts parades and public events such as the lighting of the national Christmas tree. (Constitution Ave, btwn 15th & 17th Sts NW; Ⓜ Orange, Silver, Blue Lines to Federal Triangle)

Watergate Complex NOTABLE BUILDING

4 Map p48, A3

The riverfront Watergate complex encompasses apartments, boutiques, a hotel and the office towers that made 'Watergate' a byword for political scandal after it broke that President Nixon's 'plumbers' had bugged the headquarters of the 1972 Democratic National Committee here. (2600 Virginia Ave NW; Ⓜ Orange, Silver, Blue Lines to Foggy Bottom-GWU)

Daughters of the American Revolution MUSEUM

5 Map p48, E5

The DAR's neoclassical behemoth, also known as Constitution Hall, is supposedly the largest complex of buildings in the world owned exclusively by women. They own the entire city block! Enter from D St to reach the museum, where you'll find a sweet spread of silver teapots, quilts, portrait paintings, crystal decanters and folk art. (DAR; ☏202-879-3220; www.dar.org/museum; 1776 D St NW; admission free; ⏱8:30am-4pm Mon-Fri, 9am-5pm Sat; Ⓜ Orange, Silver, Blue Lines to Farragut West)

Understand

Why Washington, DC?

Where North Meets South

Following the Revolutionary War, the fledgling US Congress set up a temporary capital in Philadelphia while searching for a more permanent home. The Constitution, ratified in 1788, specified that a federal territory, no greater than 10 sq miles, should be established for the nation's capital. Northerners and Southerners both wanted the capital in their territory, and archrivals Thomas Jefferson (a Virginian) and Alexander Hamilton (a New Yorker) struck a compromise, agreeing to construct a new city on the border between north and south. The precise location was left up to the newly inaugurated and wildly popular President George Washington.

Washington chose a site some 20 miles from his own Mount Vernon estate – a place he loved and knew well. The site on the Potomac proved a strategic location for commerce and river traffic, and was politically pleasing to both Northern and Southern concerns. Maryland and Virginia agreed to cede land to the new capital.

A Territory is Born

Over drinks at Suter's tavern in Georgetown, Washington persuaded local landowners to sell their holdings to the government for $66 an acre. In March 1791 surveyors mapped out a diamond-shaped territory that spanned the Potomac and Anacostia Rivers. Its four corners were at the cardinal points of the compass. Pierre Charles L'Enfant, a French officer in the Revolutionary War, sketched plans for a grand European-style capital of monumental buildings and majestic boulevards. It was named the Territory of Columbia (to honor Christopher Columbus), while the federal city within would be called 'the city of Washington.'

Build & Rebuild

In 1793 construction began on the President's House and the Capitol. In 1800 John Adams became the first president to occupy the mansion, and Congress convened in Washington for the first time. The new plan was going swimmingly until the War of 1812, when the British torched the city.

DC was slow to recover. A congressional initiative to abandon the dispirited capital was lost by just nine votes. It wasn't until the 1860s, when the federal government expanded to administer the Civil War and deal with its aftermath, that the city really came into its own.

Top Tip

Food Truck Fiesta

More than 150 food trucks roll in DC, and the White House neighborhood welcomes the mother lode. They congregate at Farragut Sq, Franklin Sq, the State Department and George Washington University on weekdays between 11:30am and 1:30pm. Follow the locals' lead, and stuff your face with a delicious meal for under $15 – maybe a lobster roll poached in butter or a bowl of Lao drunken noodles. **Food Truck Fiesta** (www.foodtruckfiesta.com) tracks the ever-evolving fleet via Twitter.

Eating

Founding Farmers   AMERICAN $$

6 Map p48, D3

A frosty decor of pickled goods in jars adorns this buzzy dining space. The look is a combination of rustic-cool and modern art that reflects the nature of the food: locally sourced, New American fare. Buttermilk fried chicken and waffles, and butternut squash mascarpone ravioli, are a few of the favorites that hit the wood tables. The restaurant is located in the IMF building. (📞202-822-8783; www.wearefounding farmers.com; 1924 Pennsylvania Ave NW; mains $15-28; ⏰7am-10pm Mon, 7am-11pm Tue-Thu, 7am-midnight Fri, 9am-midnight Sat, 9am-10pm Sun; 🚲; Ⓜ Orange, Silver, Blue Lines to Foggy Bottom-GWU or Farragut West)

Woodward Takeout Food   AMERICAN $

7 Map p48, G3

Woodward Takeout is the small, mostly carryout adjunct to Woodward Table, a sharp, sit-down restaurant. Go ahead: jump in the line with all the office workers angling for the duck Reuben sandwich, housemade pastrami on sourdough rye or butternut squash flatbread. It will move fast. Breakfast is busy, too, with egg-laden sandwiches on crumbly biscuits and salted chocolate croissants flying from the kitchen. (📞20 2-347-5355; http://woodwardtable.com; 1426 H St NW; mains $7-11; ⏰7:30am-4:30pm Mon-Fri; Ⓜ Orange, Silver, Blue Lines to McPherson Sq)

Old Ebbitt Grill   AMERICAN $$

8 Map p48, G3

The Grill has occupied its prime real estate, by the White House, since 1846. Political players (and lots of tourists) pack into the brass and wood interior, the sound of their conversation rumbling across a dining room where thick burgers, crab cakes and fish-and-chip type fare are rotated out almost as quickly as the clientele. Pop in for a drink and oysters during happy hour. (📞202-347-4800; www.ebbitt.com; 675 15th St NW; mains $18-28; ⏰7:30am-1am Mon-Fri, from 8:30am Sat & Sun; Ⓜ Red, Orange, Silver, Blue Lines to Metro Center)

Marcel's   FRENCH $$$

9 Map p48, B1

Marcel's keeps true to classic French cuisine while adding modern embellishments. Old school, fill-you-up-by-a-fire fare such as pork belly and turbot with peas is hearty and thick. But the sprucing on the side – quail egg and cornichons, or the miso that accompanies the Alaskan cod – is just understated enough to ratchet the experience to greatness. The menu changes daily. (☎202-296-1166; www.marcelsdc.com; 2401 Pennsylvania Ave NW; 4-/5-/7-course menus $95/115/155; ⏱5-10pm Mon-Thu, to 11pm Fri & Sat, to 9:30pm Sun; Ⓜ Orange, Silver, Blue LInes to Foggy Bottom-GWU)

BreadLine
SANDWICHES $

10 🍴 Map p48, E3

'Food is ammunition – don't waste it!' commands a WWII-era poster on the wall of BreadLine, a polished bakery and sandwich shop. Come here for a good, cheap lunch alongside local office workers. It'll probably be crowded, and with reason. The fresh sandwiches – stacked with, say, Italian sausage or barbecued vegetables on ciabatta bread – are gorgeous, as are the sweet treats. (☎202-822-8900; www.breadline.com; 1751 Pennsylvania Ave NW; sandwiches $8-12; ⏱7am-5:30pm Mon-Fri; Ⓜ Orange, Silver, Blue Lines to Farragut West)

Sichuan Pavilion
CHINESE $$

11 🍴 Map p48, D2

Many Chinese come to this unassuming restaurant to dine on fiery, oily classics of the old school. Around the world, piquant Sichuan (or Szechuan) cuisine is often blanded-up for Western customers, but these guys keep it real for all their clientele, Asian or not. The *ma-po tofu* (includes pork, fermented black beans and fiery peppercorns) is particularly stinky and sublime. (☎202-466-7790; www.sichuan-pavilion.com; 1814 K St NW; mains $15-22; ⏱11am-10pm Mon-Fri, 11:30am-9:30pm Sat & Sun; Ⓜ Orange, Silver, Blue Lines to Farragut West)

Drinking

Off The Record
BAR

12 🍺 Map p48, F2

Intimate red booths, a hidden basement location in one of the city's most prestigious hotels, right across from the White House – no wonder DC's important people submerge to be seen and not heard (as the tagline goes) at Off The Record. Experienced bartenders swirl martinis and Manhattans for the suit-wearing crowd. Groovy framed political caricatures hang on the walls. (☎202-638-6600; 800 16th St NW, Hay-Adams Hotel; ⏱11:30am-midnight Sun-Thu, to 12:30am Fri & Sat; Ⓜ Orange, Silver, Blue Lines to McPherson Sq)

Round Robin
BAR

13 🍺 Map p48, G4

Dispensing drinks since 1850, the bar at the Willard hotel is one of DC's most storied watering holes. The small, circular space is done up in Gilded Age accents, all dark wood and velvet green walls, and while it's touristy, you'll still see officials here likely determining your latest tax hike over a mint julep or single-malt Scotch. (📞202-628-9100; 1401 Pennsylvania Ave NW, Willard InterContinental Hotel; 🕐noon-1am Mon-Sat, to midnight Sun; Ⓜ Red, Orange, Silver, Blue Lines to Metro Center)

Entertainment

Kennedy Center
PERFORMING ARTS

 14 ⭐ Map p48, A4

Sprawled on 17 acres along the Potomac River, the magnificent Kennedy Center hosts a staggering array

---

☑️ **Top Tip**

Kennedy Center Freebies

Don't have the dough for a big-ticket show? No worries. Each evening the Kennedy Center's **Millennium Stage** (www.kennedy-center.org/millennium) puts on a first-rate music or dance performance at 6pm in the Grand Foyer. The cost is absolutely nada. Check the website to see who's playing.

Guides also offer free, 45-minute tours of the Kennedy's chandelier- and art-filled complex. They depart every 10 minutes from 10am to 5pm Monday to Friday and until 1pm on weekends from the tour desk on Level A, and take you into all the theaters and private lounges, as well as onto the rooftop terrace.

---

of performances – more than 2000 each year among its multiple venues including the Concert Hall (home to the National Symphony) and Opera House (home to the National Opera). A free shuttle bus runs to and from the Metro station every 15 minutes from 9:45am (noon on Sunday) to midnight. (📞202-467-4600; www.kennedy-center.org; 2700 F St NW; Ⓜ Orange, Silver, Blue Lines to Foggy Bottom-GWU)

Hamilton
LIVE MUSIC

 15 ⭐ Map p48, G3

Upstairs it's a power-player restaurant, all mahogany paneling and pork chops and silver pots of coffee. There's also a long, convivial bar with 20 beers on tap (including several local ones). Downstairs it's a 500-person live-music club that genre-jumps from funk to blues to alt-rock guitar pickers. Bands take the stage most nights of the week. (📞202-787-1000; www.thehamiltondc.com; 600 14th St NW; Ⓜ Red, Orange, Silver, Blue Lines to Metro Center)

Shopping

White House Gifts
GIFTS & SOUVENIRS

 16 🔒 Map p48, G3

Not to be confused with the official White House gift shop (in the White House Visitor Center), this store sells, er, less-official items. So while you can still find the official Christmas ornament among the stock, you'll also see

ANTON_IVANOV/SHUTTERSTOCK ©

Kennedy Center interior

caricature Trump bottle openers and the Political Inaction Figures paper doll set. (☎202-737-9500; www.white housegifts.com; 701 15th St NW; ⏰9am-8pm Mon-Sat, to 6pm Sun; Ⓜ Red, Orange, Silver, Blue Lines to Metro Center)

W Curtis Draper Tobacconist

CIGARS

17 🔒 Map p48, G3

Follow your nose into W Curtis Draper, which has been selling cigars to politicos since 1887. Make your selection, then sit in one of the overstuffed leather chairs to puff with fellow enthusiasts young and old. Staff are friendly and helpful to stogie-smoking newbies. (☎202-638-2555; www.wcurtisdraper.com; 699 15th St NW; ⏰9:30am-6:30pm Mon-Fri, 10am-5pm Sat; Ⓜ Red, Orange, Silver, Blue Lines to Metro Center)

Explore

Georgetown

Georgetown is DC's most aristocratic neighborhood, home to elite university students, ivory-tower academics and diplomats. Shopaholics have their chic boutiques lined up in a row along M St, hikers and cyclists have idyllic trails, and garden lovers have genteel landscapes to stroll through. Afterward, the upscale cafes and dark-wood pubs invite lingering into the night.

The Sights in a Day

☼ Get your garden on in the early part of the day. Amble through the exquisite blooms and art-filled mansion at **Dumbart on Oaks** (p61). Next door **Dumbarton Oaks Park** (p62) opens into creek-crossed woodlands and meadows. **Tudor Place** (p62) is another garden-mansion combination worth a look-see.

☼ Stop into **Simply Banh Mi** (p62) or **Grace Street Coffee** (p64) for an afternoon pick-me-up. Gape at the medieval-looking buildings at **Georgetown University** (p61). Stare down the **Exorcist Stairs** (p62) and be glad you're not possessed. Cycling enthusiasts can rent from **Big Wheel Bikes** (p61) and take a spin on local trails.

☽ **Key Bridge Boathouse** (p61) offers fun guided paddling tours at sunset. For dinner, munch Neapolitan pizza at cozy **Il Canale** (p63) or fork into French fare at romantic **Chez Billy Sud** (p64). Venerable **Blues Alley** (p65) books renowned jazz acts and is a fine way to end the evening.

For a local's day in Georgetown, see p58.

○ Local Life

Strolling Genteel Georgetown (p58)

♥ Best of Washington, DC

Eating

Baked & Wired (p59)

Simply Banh Mi (p62)

Fiola Mare (p63)

Sports & Activities

C&O Canal Towpath (p61)

Georgetown Waterfront Park (p59)

Key Bridge Boathouse (p61)

Dumbarton Oaks Park (p62)

Big Wheel Bikes (p61)

Getting There

Ⓜ **Metro** The Foggy Bottom-GWU stop (Orange, Silver, Blue Lines) is a 0.75-mile walk from M St's edge.

🚌 **Bus** The DC Circulator's Dupont–Georgetown–Rosslyn line runs from the Dupont Circle Metro station (south entrance), with stops along M St. The Union Station–Georgetown line runs via K St and Wisconsin Ave.

🚶 **Walk** A half-mile riverside path connects the Kennedy Center to Georgetown Waterfront Park.

Local Life
Strolling Genteel Georgetown

If ever a neighborhood was prime for ambling, it's Georgetown, in all its leafy, filigreed-manor glory. The area has always been Washington's poshest place. A wander through reveals grand row houses, swanky antique shops, indulgent patisseries and university rowing crews, along with hot spots related to John F Kennedy and Jackie.

❶ Book Hill Antiques

Book Hill is a Paris-like row of art galleries, interior-design stores and antique shops that slopes down the 1600 block of Wisconsin Ave (between Q St and R St NW). When Georgetowners need Chinese lacquered chests or lavender linen-drawer liners for their home, Book Hill is their one-stop shop.

❷ Croissants at Patisserie Poupon

The society ladies know where to replenish mid-shopping spree: **Patisserie Poupon** (📞202-342-3248; www.patisseriepoupon.net; 1645 Wisconsin Ave NW; baked goods $3-5; ⏰8:30am-6pm Tue-Fri, 8am-5:30pm Sat, 8am-4pm Sun; 🚌Circulator). Join them in nibbling almond croissants or drinking French-press coffee at one of the little cafe's tables.

❸ Martin's Tavern à la Jack & Jackie

John F Kennedy proposed to Jackie in Booth 3 at **Martin's Tavern** (📞202-333-7370; www.martinstavern.com; 1264 Wisconsin Ave NW; mains $18-32; ⏰11am-1:30am Mon-Thu, 11am-2:30am Fri, 9am-2:30am Sat, 8am-1:30am Sun; 🚌Circulator). Georgetown's oldest saloon remains a favorite with university students and senators alike, who appreciate the warm, dark-wood ambience and unfussy classics such as thick burgers, crab cakes and icy-cold beers.

❹ N Street Style

Walk on tree-shaded N St and you'll see the neighborhood's typical Federal-style row houses. With $1 million or so you can buy one of the historic beauties. JFK and Jackie lived at 3307 N St between 1958 and 1961, when they packed up and left for the White House.

❺ Drinks at the Tombs

If it looks familiar, think back to the '80s: the **Tombs** (📞202-337-6668; www.tombs.com; 1226 36th St NW; ⏰11:30am-1:30am Mon-Thu, to 2:30am Fri & Sat, 9:30am-1:30am Sun; 🚌Circulator) was the setting for the film *St Elmo's Fire*. Today the cozy, subterranean pub is a favorite with Georgetown students and teaching assistants boozing under the crew regalia affixed to the walls.

❻ M Street Shop-a-thon

M St is Georgetown's main vein where the young and fashionable come to shop. Upscale brand-name stores (AllSaints Spitalfields, Calvin Klein, Brooks Brothers) mix it up with designer consignment boutiques. Many a wallet is lightened along the way.

❼ Baked & Wired Refuel

Sniff out **Baked & Wired** (📞202-333-2500; www.bakedandwired.com; 1052 Thomas Jefferson St NW; baked goods $3-6; ⏰7am-8pm Mon-Thu, 7am-9pm Fri, 8am-9pm Sat, 8am-8pm Sun; 🚌Circulator), a cheery cafe that whips up beautifully made coffees and monster cupcakes. It's a fine spot to join students and cyclists coming off the nearby trails for a sugar buzz.

❽ People-Watching at the Park

Georgetown Waterfront Park (www.georgetownwaterfrontpark.org; Water St NW, btwn 30th St & Key Bridge; 🚌Circulator) is a favorite with couples on first dates, families on an evening stroll and power players showing off their big yachts. Benches dot the way, where you can sit and watch the rowing teams out on the Potomac River. Alfresco restaurants cluster near the harbor at 31st St NW.

For reviews see

Sights	p61
Eating	p62
Drinking	p65
Entertainment	p65
Shopping	p65

GEORGETOWN

Tudor Place 7

Dumbarton Oaks

1 19 9

17 20

14

18 16

8 Old Stone House

C&O Canal 2

Thomas Jefferson St NW

13

10

12 11

M St NW

Big Wheel Bikes 4

15

6 Exorcist Stairs

Key Bridge Boathouse 3

Whitehurst Fwy

Water St NW (underneath fwy)

Georgetown Waterfront Park

Francis Scott Key Bridge

Georgetown University 5

Foxhall Rd NW

Capital Crescent Trail

C&O Canal National Historic Park

Potomac River

Mount Vernon Trail

Theodore Roosevelt Island

WASHINGTON DC

VIRGINIA

George Washington Memorial Pkwy

500 m
0.25 miles

29th St NW
30th St NW
31st St NW
32nd St NW
Wisconsin Ave NW
33rd St NW
34th St NW
Prospect St NW
35th St NW
36th St NW
37th St NW

Q St NW
P St NW
O St NW
Dumbarton St NW
N St NW
Potomac St NW
Grace St NW
Chesapeake & Ohio Canal

Volta Pl NW

Sights

Dumbarton Oaks GARDENS, MUSEUM

1 ◉ Map p60, D1

The mansion's 10 acres of enchanting formal gardens are straight out of a storybook. In springtime, the blooms – including heaps of cherry blossoms – are stunning. The mansion itself is worth a walk-through to see exquisite Byzantine and pre-Columbian art (including El Greco's *The Visitation*) and the fascinating library of rare books. (📞202-339-6401; www.doaks.org; 1703 32nd St NW; museum free, gardens adult/child $10/5; ⊙museum 11:30am-5:30pm Tue-Sun, gardens 2-6pm; 🚌Circulator)

C&O Canal Towpath CYCLING

2 ◉ Map p60, E3

The shaded hiking-cycling path – part of a larger national historic park – runs alongside a waterway constructed in the mid-1800s to transport goods all the way to West Virginia. The canal and environs are being restored and enhanced into mid-2018, but once the work is finished, you can step on at Jefferson St for a lovely green escape from the crowd. (www.nps.gov/choh; 1057 Thomas Jefferson St NW; 🚌Circulator)

Key Bridge Boathouse KAYAKING

3 ◉ Map p60, C3

Located beneath the Key Bridge, the boathouse rents canoes, kayaks and stand-up paddleboards (prices start at $16 per hour). In summer, it also offers guided, 90-minute kayak trips ($45 per person) that glide past the Lincoln Memorial as the sun sets. If you have a bike, the boathouse is a mere few steps from the Capital Crescent Trail. (📞20 2-337-9642; www.boatingindc.com/boathous es/key-bridge-boathouse; 3500 Water St NW; ⊙hours vary mid-Apr–Oct; 🚌Circulator)

Big Wheel Bikes CYCLING

4 ◉ Map p60, C3

Big Wheel has a wide variety of two-wheelers to rent, and you can spin onto the C&O Canal Towpath practically from the front door. Staff members also provide the lowdown on the nearby **Capital Crescent Trail** (www.cctrail.org; Water St) and Mount Vernon Trail. There's a three-hour minimum with rentals. For an extra $10 you can keep your bike overnight. (📞202-337-0254; www.bigwheelbikes. com; 1034 33rd St NW; per 3hr/day $21/35; ⊙11am-7pm Tue-Fri, 10am-6pm Sat & Sun; 🚌Circulator)

Georgetown University UNIVERSITY

5 ◉ Map p60, B2

Georgetown is one of the nation's top universities, with a student body that's equally hard-working and hard-partying. Founded in 1789, it was America's first Roman Catholic university. Notable Hoya (derived from the Latin *hoya saxa,* 'what rocks') alumni include Bill Clinton, as well as many international royals and heads of state. Near the campus' east gate, medieval-looking

Healy Hall impresses with its tall, Hogwarts-esque clock tower. Pretty Dalghren Chapel and its quiet courtyard hide behind it. (202-687-0100; www.georgetown.edu; cnr 37th & O Sts NW; Circulator)

Exorcist Stairs   FILM LOCATION

6 Map p60, C3

The steep set of stairs dropping down to M St is a popular track for joggers, but more famously it's the spot where demonically possessed Father Karras tumbles to his death in horror-film classic *The Exorcist* (1973). Come on foggy nights, when the stone steps really are creepy as hell. (3600 Prospect St NW; Circulator)

Tudor Place   MUSEUM

7 Map p60, D1

This 1816 neoclassical mansion was owned by Thomas Peter and Martha

Local Life
Dumbarton Oaks Park
Next door to Dumbarton Oaks garden, **Dumbarton Oaks Park** (www.dopark.org; Lovers' Lane; sunrisesunset; Circulator) was once part of the estate but is now a public woodland beloved by joggers and dog walkers. Access it via Lovers' Lane (a paved path 200ft east of R and 31st Sts) and enter a world of forested trails, quaint stone bridges, mini waterfalls and deerfilled meadows.

Custis Peter, the granddaughter of Martha Washington. Today the mansion functions as a small museum, featuring furnishings and artwork from Mount Vernon, which give good insight into American decorative arts. The grand, 5-acre gardens bloom with roses, lilies, poplar trees and exotic palms. (20 2-965-0400; www.tudorplace.org; 1644 31st St NW; 1hr house tour adult/child $10/3, self-guided garden tour $3; 10am-4pm Tue-Sat, from noon Sun, closed Jan; Circulator)

Old Stone House   HISTORIC SITE

8 Map p60, E3

Built in 1765, the capital's oldest surviving building has been a tavern, a brothel and a boardinghouse (sometimes all at once). Today it's a small museum offering a peek into Revolutionary War–era life. The evocative little garden in back is worth a mosey. (www.nps.gov/olst; 3051 M St NW; admission free; 11am-6pm; Circulator)

Eating

Simply Banh Mi   VIETNAMESE $

9 Map p60, D1

There's nothing fancy about the small, below-street-level space, and the compact menu sticks mostly to sandwiches and bubble tea. But the brother-sister owners know how to take a crusty baguette, stuff it with delicious lemongrass pork or other meat (or tofu), and make your day. They're super attentive to quality and to customer needs (vegan, gluten free etc).

IAN DAGNALL COMMERCIAL COLLECTION/ALAMY STOCK PHOTO ©

Old Stone House

(📞202-333-5726; www.simplybanhmidc.com; 1624 Wisconsin Ave NW; mains $7-10; ⏱11am-7pm Tue-Sun; 🖉; 🚌Circulator)

Il Canale
ITALIAN $$

10 🍴 Map p60, E3

Real-deal Neapolitan pizza emerges from the real-deal, Italian wood-fired oven in Il Canale's bouncy townhouse digs. It's casual and low-cost for Georgetown, which is why families, couples and groups of friends pile in at all hours. The calamari, lasagna, pastas and cannoli are all crowd pleasers. (📞202-337-4444; www.ilcanale.com; 1063 31st St NW; mains $19-25; ⏱11:30am-10:30pm Mon-Thu, 11am-11pm Fri & Sat, 11am-10pm Sun; 🚌Circulator)

Fiola Mare
SEAFOOD $$$

11 🍴 Map p60, E4

Fiola Mare delivers the chi-chi Georgetown experience. It flies in fresh fish and crustaceans from Maine to Tasmania daily. The yacht-bobbling river view rocks. The see-and-be-seen multitudes are here. It's DC at its luxe best. Try it at lunchtime on a weekday, when $24 gets you an Italian-style seafood main and a drink in the bar area. Best make reservations. (📞202-628-0065; www.fiolamaredc.com; 3050 K St NW; mains $28-50; ⏱5-10pm Mon, 11:30am-2:30pm & 5-10pm Tue-Fri, 11:30am-2pm & 5-10:30pm Sat, 11am-2pm & 5-10pm Sun; 🚌Circulator)

Chez Billy Sud

FRENCH $$$

12 Map p60, E3

An endearing little bistro tucked away on a residential block, Billy's mint-green walls, gilt mirrors and wee marble bar exude laid-back elegance. Mustachioed servers bring baskets of warm bread to the white linen–clothed tables, along with crackling pork and pistachio sausage, golden trout, tuna niçoise salad and plump cream puffs. (202-965-2606; www.chezbillysud.com; 1039 31st St NW; mains $26-37; 11:30am-2pm Tue-Fri, 11am-2pm Sat & Sun, plus 5-10pm Tue-Thu & Sun, 5-11pm Fri & Sat; Circulator)

Unum

AMERICAN $$

13 Map p60, E3

Unum hops on the upscale-casual, modern-American-fare bandwagon

with its shareable plates and mains (most of which are available by the half-order) such as Indian-spiced lamb shank and kale-pesto-sauced goat cheese ravioli. Sides of cashew-raisin Brussels sprouts and lots of California wines go alongside. The intimate room, glimmering in warm golds and light wood, will please romantics. (202-621-6959; www.unumdc.com; 2917 M St NW; mains $21-28; 5:30-10pm Mon-Thu, to 11pm Fri & Sat, to 9pm Sun; Circulator)

Cafe Milano

ITALIAN $$$

14 Map p60, D2

Milano has been reeling in the political glitterati and besotted Georgetown couples for years with its executions of northern Italian favorites. Be prepared to pay for the European-chic ambience and celebrity-spotting. The pastas get the biggest praise. (202-333-6183; www.cafemilano.com; 3251 Prospect St NW; mains $25-45; 11:30am-11pm Mon & Tue, to midnight Wed-Sat, 11am-11pm Sun; Circulator)

Pie Sisters

BAKERY $

15 Map p60, C3

The neighbors can't help but stop in to see what the Pie Sisters have cooling on the rack. Chocolate cream and jumbleberry tempt among the sweet wares, while chicken pot pie and pork barbecue pie waft savory goodness. The sweet ones come in bite-size and cupcake-size versions, but go for a full slice for best results. (202-338-7437; www.piesisters.com; 3423 M St NW; slices $5-6; 11am-6pm Wed-Sun; Circulator)

Drinking

Ching Ching Cha TEAHOUSE

16 Map p60, D3

Airy, Zen-like Ching Ching Cha is a world away from the shopping mayhem of M St. Stop in for a leisurely pot of rare tea (it brews more than 70 varieties) and snacks such as steamed dumplings, coconut tarts, or a 'tea meal,' with three little dishes along the lines of green squash and miso salmon. (☏202-333-8288; www.chingchingcha.com; 1063 Wisconsin Ave NW; ⊙11am-9pm Tue-Sun; ☐Circulator)

Cafe Bonaparte CAFE

17 Map p60, D1

This jewel-box cafe feels as though it has been plucked straight from the streets of Paris. Come to sip a *cafe au lait* or a glass of sparkling wine. Hopefully you're not in a hurry, because service can be slow. Frites, crepes and chocolate tortes emerge from the kitchen for those in need of a nosh. (☏202-333-8830; www.cafebonaparte.com; 1522 Wisconsin Ave NW; ⊙9am-11pm Mon-Fri, 10am-11pm Sat, 9am-10pm Sun; ☐Circulator)

Entertainment

Blues Alley JAZZ

18 Map p60, D3

Greats like Dizzy Gillespie and Sarah Vaughan played this venerable club back in the day. The talent remains just as sterling now, and the setting just as sophisticated. Reserve a ticket in advance if a big name is making music. Enter through the alley just off M St, south of Wisconsin Ave. There's a $12 food or beverage minimum purchase requirement once you're seated. (☏202-337-4141; www.bluesalley.com; 1073 Wisconsin Ave NW; tickets from $20; ⊙shows 8pm & 10pm; ☐Circulator)

Shopping

Oliver Dunn, Moss & Co ANTIQUES

19 Map p60, D1

The lengthy name comes from two businesses under one roof. Located in a cute row house in the thick of Book Hill (Georgetown's antique-laden block of shops), this spot spreads posh linens, Scandinavian textiles, French signs and concrete garden ornaments through six rooms and into the back yard. (☏202-338-7410; 1657 Wisconsin Ave NW; ⊙11am-5pm Tue-Sat; ☐Circulator)

Tugooh Toys TOYS

20 Map p60, D2

If you've ever been nostalgic for the great wooden toys of childhood, this hip wonderland has the goods with clever modern touches. Lots of eco-friendly playthings (ie cuddly animals made with high-quality organic cotton) and educational games stack the shelves, too. (☏202-338-9476; www.tugoohtoys.com; 1355 Wisconsin Ave NW; ⊙10am-6pm; ☐Circulator)

Explore

Capitol Hill

The city's geographic and legislative heart surprises by being mostly a row-house-lined residential neighborhood. The vast area holds top sights such as the big domed Capitol and US Holocaust Memorial Museum, but creaky bookshops and cozy pubs also thrive here. The areas around Eastern Market and H St NE are locals' hubs, with good-time restaurants and nightlife.

The Sights in a Day

 Tour the dramatic **Capitol** (p68; pictured left), filled with statues, frescoes and whispery chambers. Take the underground tunnel over to the **Supreme Court** (p76). Hopefully the justices are listening to oral arguments (October to April) that you can sit in on; otherwise you're free to explore the building. Next door the **Library of Congress** (p76) holds fascinating exhibits and artworks.

Get lunch fresh off the boat at the **Maine Avenue Fish Market** (p78). The haunting **United States Holocaust Memorial Museum** (p70) and money-churning **Bureau of Engraving & Printing** (p77) sit side by side in a little sliver of spillover from the Mall.

When the sun goes down, head to H St NE. Have dinner at **Toki Underground** (p78) or **Ethiopic** (p78), booze at **Copycat Co** (p79) or **Little Miss Whiskey's Golden Dollar** (p79), and catch a set at the **Rock & Roll Hotel** (p81). Another option is to spend the evening at **Nationals Park** (p81), with a pit stop at **Bluejacket Brewery** (p79) or **Bardo Brewing** (p81).

For a local's day in Capitol Hill, see p72.

 Top Sight

Capitol (p68)

United States Holocaust Memorial Museum (p70)

 Local Life

A Capital Day on Capitol Hill (p72)

💜 **Best of Washington, DC**

Eating

Rose's Luxury (p73)

Maine Avenue Fish Market (p78)

Ted's Bulletin (p78)

Bars & Clubs

Copycat Co (p79)

Bluejacket Brewery (p79)

Tune Inn (p72)

Getting There

Ⓜ **Metro** Union Station (Red Line), Capitol South (Orange, Silver and Blue), Eastern Market (Orange, Silver and Blue) and Navy Yard (Green) are the main stations.

🚋 **Streetcar** DC's free new line zips along H St from Union Station to 15th St. Catch it behind Union Station (follow the streetcar signs through the terminal, past all the buses).

Top Sights
Capitol

The political center of the US government and geographic heart of the District, the Capitol sits atop a high hill overlooking the National Mall and the wide avenues flaring out to the city beyond. The towering 288ft cast-iron dome, ornate fountains and marble Roman pillars set on sweeping lawns scream: 'This is DC.'

👁 Map p74, D3

www.visitthecapitol.gov

1st St NE & E Capitol St

admission free

🕗 8:30am-4:30pm Mon-Sat

Ⓜ Orange, Silver, Blue Lines to Capitol South

The Capitol's Rotunda

Capitol Visitor Center & Tours

The Capitol Visitor Center sits below the East Plaza and is where all visits begin. Tours are free, but you need a ticket. Get one at the information desk, or reserve online in advance (there's no fee). The hour-long jaunt starts with a cheesy film about how the US government works. Then staff members lead you into the ornate halls and whispery chambers.

Rotunda

The Capitol's centerpiece is the magnificent Rotunda (the area under the dome). It's 96ft in diameter and 180ft high. A Constantino Brumidi frieze around the rim replays more than 400 years of American history. Look up into the eye of the dome for the *Apotheosis of Washington,* an allegorical fresco by Brumidi.

Statues

The Capitol also contains sculptures of two famous residents per state. Many of these are found in the Hall of Statues. You might recognize likenesses of George Washington (Virginia) and Ronald Reagan (California), less so Uriah Milton Rose (Arkansas). After the tour, swing by the Exhibition Hall and check out the plaster model for the *Statue of Freedom* that crowns the dome.

Military Bands

The Army, Navy, Marine Corps and Air Force bands take turns performing on the steps of the Capitol on weekdays (except Thursday) June through August. Look for them at 8pm on the West Front.

☑ Top Tips

▶ Between March and August, it's wise to reserve tours online in advance (there's no fee).

▶ Note you cannot bring any food or drinks inside the building.

▶ The Visitor Center offers several free apps that provide details on the Capitol grounds and more. Download them at www.visitthecapitol.gov/apps.

▶ To reach the Supreme Court and Library of Congress easily, take the underground tunnel from the Capitol.

✕ Take a Break

Jimmy T's (☏202-546-3646; 501 E Capitol St SE; mains $6-10; ⊗6:30am-3pm Tue-Fri, from 8am Sat & Sun; ⓜOrange, Silver, Blue Lines to Eastern Market) is an old-school diner, four blocks from the Capitol, where locals come for omelets and coffee; cash only.

Good Stuff Eatery (p79) is also nearby for foodie-style burgers and milk shakes.

Top Sights
United States Holocaust Memorial Museum

For a deep understanding of the Holocaust, this harrowing museum is a must-see. It gives visitors the identity card of a single Holocaust victim, whose story gets revealed as you plunge into a past marked by ghettos, rail cars and death camps. It also shows the flip side of human nature, documenting the risks many citizens took to help the persecuted.

◉ Map p74, A3

www.ushmm.org

100 Raoul Wallenberg Pl SW

🕒 10am–5:20pm, extended hours Apr–mid-Jun

🚌 Circulator, Ⓜ Orange, Silver, Blue Lines to Smithsonian

Hall of Remembrance

Hall of Witness & Skylight

James Ingo Freed designed the extraordinary building in 1993, and its stark facade and steel-and-glass interior echo the death camps themselves. Look up at the skylight in the Hall of Witness when you enter the building. Many survivors say this reminds them of the sky above the camps. For them it was symbolic, the only thing the Nazis couldn't control.

Nazi Assault

The permanent exhibit presents the Holocaust's history chronologically in galleries spanning three floors. It starts on the 4th floor, which is titled 'Nazi Assault' and covers the period between 1933 and 1939. Watch propaganda films of Hitler, Goebbels and others, and learn how the Nazis used then modern technology, such as film, to craft their message to sway citizens.

Final Solution & Last Chapter

The 3rd floor is 'The Final Solution,' covering the period between 1940 and 1945. Here you'll see a rail car used to transport people to the camps, a wooden bunk bed from Auschwitz and a scale model of Crematorium II at Auschwitz. The 2nd floor is the 'Last Chapter,' where old film footage shows their liberation from camps, and videos illuminate individual survivors telling their stories.

Hall of Remembrance & Wexner Center

As you exit the permanent exhibit, you come out into the candlelit Hall of Remembrance, a sanctuary for quiet reflection. The Wexner Center is likewise on this floor, and features exhibits on other genocides around the world.

☑ Top Tips

▶ Same-day passes to view the permanent exhibit are required March through August, available at the pass desk on the 1st floor. The passes allow entrance at a designated time. Arrive early because they do run out.

▶ Better yet, reserve tickets in advance via the museum's website for a $1 surcharge.

▶ If you have children under 11 years, a gentler installation – 'Remember the Children: Daniel's Story' – is on the 1st floor.

✖ Take a Break

Follow your nose to the Maine Avenue Fish Market (p78) and a feast of blue crabs and chowder. It's about 0.75 miles southeast of the museum.

Hop on the Metro to Eastern Market (p73), where cheese, fruit, baked goods and other picnic fixings await.

Local Life
A Capital Day on Capitol Hill

Pretend you're a resident of one of the brownstone homes along the red-brick sidewalks and shop for seafood at Eastern Market or browse the Flea Market's curios. Have breakfast anytime in a dive bar, then stop by the rambling, double-stacked bookshop. Share small plates and drinks with friends, and wave to neighbors at the riverside park.

....

1 **The Dive Bar:**
Tune Inn

Tune Inn (☎202-543-2725; 331 Pennsylvania Ave SE; ⊗8am-2am Sun-Thu, to 3am Fri & Sat; Ⓜ Orange, Silver, Blue Lines to Capitol South or Eastern Market) has been around for decades and is where the neighborhood's older residents come to down Budweisers. The mounted deer heads and antler chandelier set the mood, as all-day breakfasts get gobbled in the vinyl-backed booths.

❷ Capitol Hill Books

Rambling **Capitol Hill Books** (📞202-544-1621; www.capitolhillbooks-dc.com; 657 C St SE; ⏰11:30am-6pm Mon-Fri, from 9am Sat & Sun; Ⓜ Orange, Silver, Blue Lines to Eastern Market) has so many used tomes they're stacked two deep on the shelves. They're even stacked in the bathroom. Floors creak and classical music plays as neighborhood bibliophiles sift through the whopping selection.

❸ Eastern Market

Eastern Market (📞202-698-5253; www.easternmarket-dc.org; 225 7th St SE; ⏰7am-7pm Tue-Fri, to 6pm Sat, 9am-5pm Sun; Ⓜ Orange, Silver, Blue Lines to Eastern Market) is the true heart of Capitol Hill. Vendors selling baked goods, cheeses, meats, seafood and produce fill the covered arcade. It's not that large... until the weekend, when artisans and farmers join the fun and the market spills onto the street.

❹ Flea Market Finds

On weekends the **Flea Market** (www.easternmarket.net; 7th St SE, btwn C St and Penn Ave; ⏰10am-5pm Sat & Sun; Ⓜ Orange, Silver, Blue Lines to Eastern Market) sets up in the street adjacent to Eastern Market, doubling the browsing acreage. Vendors sell cool art, antiques, furniture, maps, prints, global wares, clothing and curios. Sunday is the busier day, with more stalls.

❺ Street Art at the Fridge

First you have to find **The Fridge** (📞202-664-4151; www.thefridgedc.com; 516½ 8th St SE, rear alley; admission free; ⏰noon-8pm Wed-Sat, to 5pm Sun; Ⓜ Orange, Silver, Blue Lines to Eastern Market), a friendly gallery specializing in street art. Follow the murals into the alley beside Senart's oyster house on 8th St. Opening times can be erratic, but at least you'll see lots of street art en route.

❻ Meet Friends at Ambar

Ambar (📞202-813-3039; www.ambarrestaurant.com; 523 8th St SE; small plates $7-13; ⏰11am-2pm & 4-10pm Mon-Thu, to 11pm Fri, 10am-11pm Sat, 10am-10pm Sun; Ⓜ Orange, Silver, Blue Lines to Eastern Market) buzzes, especially at happy hour, when the convivial restaurant slings heaps of small plates. Roasted pepper and eggplant, lamb salami, brandy-soaked mussels – tables of friends share intriguing Balkan dishes (alongside drinks, of course).

❼ Dinner at Rose's Luxury

Locals line up for shabby-chic **Rose's Luxury** (📞202-580-8889; www.roseluxury.com; 717 8th St SE; small plates $13-16, family-style plates $28-33; ⏰5-10pm Mon-Sat; Ⓜ Orange, Silver, Blue Lines to Eastern Market), which offers a small, changing menu of 10 or so plates a day. The pork sausage, habanero and lychee salad is the salty-sweet dish on everyone's lips.

❽ River Views at Yards Park

Lovely **Yards Park** (www.capitolriverfront.org/yards-park; 355 Water St SE; ⏰7am-2hr past sunset; Ⓜ Green Line to Navy Yard) is a sculpted public space with a wooden boardwalk, excellent river views, a funky modernist bridge and a mini tidal pool that is popular with neighborhood families on summer evenings.

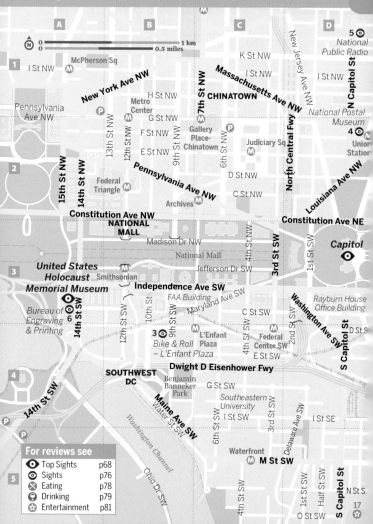

A | B | C | D

1

I St NW

McPherson Sq

5
National
Public Radio

I St NW

New York Ave NW

K St NW

New Jersey Ave NW

Massachusetts Ave NW

I St NW

I St NW

N Capitol St

Pennsylvania
Ave NW

H St NW

Metro
Center

CHINATOWN

G St NW

F St NW

13th St NW

12th St NW

7th St NW

9th St NW

Gallery
Place-
Chinatown

6th St NW

Judiciary Sq

National Postal
Museum

4
Union
Station

E St NW

2

15th St NW

14th St NW

Federal
Triangle

Pennsylvania Ave NW

D St NW

C St NW

North Central Fwy

Louisiana Ave NW

Archives

Constitution Ave NW
**NATIONAL
MALL**

Madison Dr NW

National Mall

3rd St SW

4th St SW

1st St SW

Constitution Ave NE

Capitol

3

**United States
Holocaust
Memorial Museum**

Smithsonian

Independence Ave SW

Jefferson Dr SW

FAA Building

Maryland Ave SW

C St SW

Washington Ave SW

Rayburn House
Office Building

D St S

*Bureau of
Engraving
& Printing*

14th St SW

6

12th St SW

10th St

9th St SW

3
Bike & Roll
– L'Enfant Plaza

L'Enfant
Plaza

4th St SW

Federal
Center SW

2nd St SW

E St SW

S Capitol St

Dwight D Eisenhower Fwy

4

14th St SW

**SOUTHWEST
DC**

Benjamin
Banneker
Park

Maine Ave SW

G St SW

Southeastern
University

I St SW

Water St SW

6th St SW

3rd St SW

Delaware Ave SW

I St SE

Washington Channel

Waterfront

M St SW

5

Ohio Dr SW

4th St SW

1st St SW

Half St SW

S Capitol St

N St SE

17

O St SW

For reviews see

◉ Top Sights	p68
◉ Sights	p76
🍴 Eating	p78
🍷 Drinking	p79
★ Entertainment	p81

Sights

Library of Congress
LIBRARY

1 Map p74, E3

The world's largest library – with 164 million books, manuscripts, maps, photos, films and other items – awes in both scope and design. The centerpiece is the 1897 Jefferson Building. Gawk at the Great Hall, done up in stained glass, marble and mosaics of mythical characters, then seek out the Gutenberg Bible (c 1455), Thomas Jefferson's round library and the reading room viewing area. Free tours of the building take place between 10:30am and 3:30pm on the half-hour. (☏202-707-8000; www.loc.gov; 1st St SE; admission free; ☺8:30am-4:30pm Mon-Sat; Ⓜ Orange, Silver, Blue Lines to Capitol South)

Supreme Court
LANDMARK

2 Map p74, E3

The highest court in the USA sits in a pseudo-Greek temple protected by 13,000lb bronze doors. Arrive early to watch arguments (periodic Monday through Wednesday October to April). You can visit the permanent exhibits and the building's five-story, marble-and-bronze, spiral staircase year-round. On days when court is not in session you also can hear lectures (every hour on the half-hour) in the courtroom. When departing, be sure to exit via the doors that lead to the regal front steps. (☏202-479-3030; www.supremecourt.gov; 1 1st St NE; admission free; ☺9am-4:30pm Mon-Fri; Ⓜ Orange, Silver, Blue Lines to Capitol South)

Bike & Roll – L'Enfant Plaza
CYCLING

3 Map p74, B4

This branch of the bike-rental company (from $16 per two hours) is the one closest to the Mall. In addition to bike rental, it also provides tours. Three-hour jaunts wheel by the main sights of Capitol Hill and the National Mall. The evening rides to the monuments are particularly good. (☏20 2-842-2453; www.bikeandrolldc.com; 955 L'Enfant Plaza SW; tours adult/child $45/35; ☺mid-Mar–early Dec; Ⓜ Orange, Silver, Blue, Yellow, Green Lines to L'Enfant Plaza)

National Postal Museum
MUSEUM

4 Map p74, D2

The Smithsonian-run Postal Museum is way cooler than you might think. Level 1 has exhibits on postal history, where you'll see antique mail planes and touching old letters from soldiers and pioneers. Level 2 holds the world's largest stamp collection. Join the stamp geeks pulling out drawers and snapping photos of the world's rarest stamps (the Ben Franklin Z Grill!), or start your own collection, choosing from among thousands of free international stamps (Guyana, Congo, Cambodia...). (☏20 2-633-5555; www.postalmuseum.si.edu; 2 Massachusetts Ave NE; admission free; ☺10am-5:30pm; Ⓜ Red Line to Union Station)

FUJIPHOTO/SHUTTERSTOCK ©

Library of Congress

National Public Radio

NOTABLE BUILDING

5 🎯 Map p74, D1

Fans of *Morning Edition* and *All Things Considered* can see where the magic happens at National Public Radio's ecofriendly headquarters. Hour-long tours peek into the newsroom and a high-tech production studio. The guides – usually former employees – entertain with insider stories. Reservations required. The on-site shop sells nifty gifts such as the Nina Totin' bag (named for longtime reporter Nina Totenberg). (📞202-513-2000; www.npr.org/about-npr/177066727/visit-npr; 1111 N Capitol St NE; admission free; ⊙tours 11am Mon-Fri; Ⓜ Red Line to NoMa)

Bureau of Engraving & Printing

LANDMARK

6 🎯 Map p74, A3

The nation's paper currency is designed and printed here. Guides lead 40-minute tours during which you peer down onto the work floor where millions of dollars roll off the presses and get cut (by guillotine!). In peak season (March to August), timed entry tickets are required. Get in line early at the **ticket kiosk** (Raoul Wallenberg Pl, ⊙from 8am) as tickets are often gone by 10am. (📞202-874-2330; www.moneyfactory.gov; cnr 14th & C Sts SW; admission free; ⊙9-10:45am, 12:30-3:45pm & 5-6pm Mon-Fri Mar-Aug, reduced hours Sep-Feb; 🚌Circulator, Ⓜ Orange, Silver, Blue Lines to Smithsonian)

Local Life

Maine Avenue Fish Market

The pungent, open-air **Maine Avenue Fish Market** (1100 Maine Ave SW; mains $7-13; ⏱8am-9pm; **M**Orange, Silver, Blue, Yellow, Green Lines to L'Enfant Plaza) is a local landmark. No-nonsense vendors sell fish, crabs, oysters and other seafood so fresh it's almost still flopping. They'll kill, strip, shell, gut, and fry or broil your desire, which you can take to the waterfront benches and eat blissfully (mind the seagulls!).

Eating

Toki Underground   ASIAN $

7   Map p74, G1

Spicy ramen noodles and dumplings sum up wee Toki's menu. The eatery takes limited reservations, so there's typically a wait. Use the opportunity to explore the surrounding bars; Toki will text when your table is ready. The restaurant isn't signposted; look for the Pug bar, and Toki is above it. (☑202-388-3086; www.tokiunderground.com; 1234 H St NE; mains $13-15; ⏱11:30am-2:30pm & 5-10pm Mon-Thu, to midnight Fri & Sat; **M**Red Line to Union Station then streetcar)

Ethiopic   ETHIOPIAN $$

8   Map p74, E1

In a city with no shortage of Ethiopian joints, Ethiopic stands above the rest. Top marks go to the various *wats* (stews) and the signature *tibs* (sauteed meat and veg), derived from tender lamb that has sat in a bath of herbs and hot spices. Vegans get lots of love here. (☑202-675-2066; www.ethiopicrestaurant.com; 401 H St NE; mains $13-19; ⏱5-10pm Tue-Thu, from noon Fri-Sun; ☑; **M**Red Line to Union Station)

Pineapple and Pearls   AMERICAN $$$

9 ✗ Map p74, F4

By day it's a takeaway-only coffee bar pumping out lattes to go with eclectic treats (think pink peppercorn short-bread cookies and pistachio rose tea cake). At night it's a kicky restaurant that has a pair of Michelin stars and features a 13-course tasting menu of wild takes on comfort foods. (☑202-595-7375; www.pineappleandpearls.com; 715 8th St SE; pastries $2-4, 13-course tasting menu $180-280; ⏱coffee bar 8am-2pm Tue-Fri, to 4pm Sat, dinner seatings 5pm & 8:15pm Tue-Sat; **M**Orange, Silver, Blues Lines to Eastern Market)

Ted's Bulletin   AMERICAN $$

10 ✗ Map p74, F4

Plop into a booth in the art-deco-meets-diner ambience, and loosen the belt. Beer biscuits and sausage gravy for breakfast other hipster spins on comfort foods hit the table. You've got to admire a place that lets you substitute pop tarts for toast. Breakfast is available all day. (☑202-544-8337; www.tedsbulletincapitolhill.com; 505 8th St SE; mains $11-19; ⏱7am-10:30pm Sun-Thu, to 11:30pm Fri & Sat; **M**Orange, Silver, Blue Lines to Eastern Market)

Le Grenier FRENCH $$

11 Map p74, F1

This romantic French bistro, set in an exposed brick row house checks all the boxes: buttery escargot, rich cheese plates, great wines, vintage Left Bank ambience. Order a sparking aperitif, a saucy mushroom crepe or the beef bourguignon and pretend you're across the Atlantic. (☏202-544-4999; www.legrenierdc.com; 502 H St NE; mains $18-26; ☺5-10pm Tue-Thu, 5-11pm Fri, 11am-11pm Sat, 11am-10pm Sun; Ⓜ Red Line to Union Station then DC Streetcar)

Good Stuff Eatery BURGERS $

12 Map p74, E3

A popular burgers-shakes-and-fries spot, you can top off fries at the 'dipping bar' of various sauces, and the toasted-marshmallow milkshake comes with an honest-to-god toasted marshmallow. The ambience is that of a fast-food joint, and seats are at a premium weekend nights, when Cap Hill youth descend on the place. (☏202-543-8222; www.goodstuffeatery.com; 303 Pennsylvania Ave SE; burgers $7-9; ☺11am-10pm Mon-Sat; Ⓜ Orange, Silver, Blue Lines to Capitol South or Eastern Market)

Drinking

Copycat Co COCKTAIL BAR

13 Map p74, G1

When you walk into Copycat it feels like a Chinese fast-food restaurant. That's because it is (sort of) on the 1st floor, where Chinese-street-food nibbles are available. The fizzy drinks and egg-white-topped cocktails fill glasses upstairs, in the dimly lit, speakeasy-meets-opium-den-vibed bar. Staff are unassuming and gracious in helping newbies figure out what they want from the lengthy menu. (☏202-241-1952; www.copycatcompany.com; 1110 H St NE; ☺5pm-2am Sun-Thu, to 3am Fri & Sat; Ⓜ Red Line to Union Station then DC Streetcar)

Bluejacket Brewery BREWERY

14 Map p74, E5

Beer-lovers' heads will explode in Bluejacket. Pull up a stool at the mod-industrial bar, gaze at the silvery tanks bubbling up the ambitious brews, then make the hard decision about which of the 25 tap beers you want to try. Four-ounce tasting pours

Local Life

Seventh Hill Pizza

It's just blistered, thin-crust pizza, but it's soooo addictive, which is why neighbors hobnob at **Seventh Hill Pizza** (☏202-544-1911; www.montmartredc.com/seventhhill; 327 7th St SE; pizzas $11-17; ☺11:30am-2:30pm & 5-10pm Tue-Fri, 11:30am-10pm Sat, noon-9pm Sun; Ⓜ Orange, Silver, Blue Lines to Eastern Market). Each pie is named for a local street or park, like the 'Potomac Ave,' topped with Felino salami and arugula, or the 'Maryland Ave' with egg, pesto and pecorino. Good French wines accompany the wares.

Understand

Slave to Statesman: Frederick Douglass

Born Frederick Augustus Washington Bailey in 1818 on a slave plantation along Maryland's Eastern Shore, Frederick Douglass is remembered as one of the country's most influential and outstanding black 19th-century leaders.

In 1838, at 20 years old, he escaped wretched treatment at the hands of Maryland planters and established himself as a freeman in New Bedford, Massachusetts, eventually working for abolitionist William Lloyd Garrison's antislavery paper, the *Liberator*. After his escape, he took his new last name from a character in the Sir Walter Scott book *The Lady of the Lake*. Largely self-educated, Douglass had a natural gift for eloquence. In 1841 he won the admiration of New England abolitionists with an impromptu speech at an antislavery convention, introducing himself as 'a recent graduate from the institution of slavery,' with his 'diploma' (ie whip marks on his back).

Crusader & Underground Railroad Conductor

Douglass' effectiveness so angered proslavery forces that his supporters urged him to flee to England to escape seizure and punishment under the Fugitive Slave Law. He followed their advice and kept lecturing in England until admirers contributed enough money ($710.96) to enable him to purchase his freedom and return home in 1847.

Douglass then became the self-proclaimed station master and conductor of the Underground Railroad in Rochester, NY, working with other famed abolitionists such as Harriet Tubman and John Brown. In 1860 Douglass campaigned for Abraham Lincoln, and when the Civil War broke out, helped raise two regiments of black soldiers – the Massachusetts 54th and 55th – to fight for the Union.

Postwar Leader

After the war, Douglass went to Washington to lend his support to the 13th, 14th and 15th Constitutional Amendments, which abolished slavery, granted citizenship to former slaves and guaranteed citizens the right to vote.

In 1895 Douglass died at his Anacostia home, Cedar Hill, now the Frederick Douglass National Historic Site. The hilltop residence sits just across the Anacostia River, about 2 miles southeast of Nationals Park.

help with decision-making. (☎202-524-4862; www.bluejacketdc.com; 300 Tingey St SE; ⏰11am-1am Sun-Thu, to 2am Fri & Sat; Ⓜ Green Line to Navy Yard)

Granville Moore's
PUB

15 🍺 Map p74, G1

Besides being one of DC's best places to grab frites and a steak sandwich, Granville Moore's has an extensive Belgian beer menu that should satisfy any fan of low-country boozing. With its raw, wooden fixtures, the interior resembles a medieval barracks. The fireside setting is ideal on a winter's eve. (☎202-399-2546; www.granville moores.com; 1238 H St NE; ⏰5pm-midnight Mon-Thu, 5pm-3am Fri, 11am-3am Sat, 11am-midnight Sun; Ⓜ Red Line to Union Station then streetcar)

Little Miss Whiskey's Golden Dollar
BAR

If Alice had returned from Wonderland so traumatized by her near beheading that she needed a stiff drink, we imagine she'd pop down to Little Miss Whiskey's (see 13 🍺 Map p74; G1). She'd love the whimsical-meets-dark-nightmares decor. She'd also adore the weirdly fantastic back patio. (www. littlemisswhiskeys.com; 1104 H St NE; ⏰5pm-2am Sun-Thu, to 3am Fri & Sat; Ⓜ Red Line to Union Station then streetcar)

Bardo Brewing
BEER GARDEN

16 🍺 Map p74, E5

Sprawled by the river in the shadow of Nationals Park, Bardo is part

beer garden with picnic tables, part brewpub, part dog park and part cornhole sportsplex. It rarely feels crowded (because it's huge), and almost always is relaxed with bearded types hobnobbing over beers. The suds tend toward brawny stouts and India Pale Ales. (www.bardo.beer; 25 Potomac Ave SE; ⏰5pm-midnight Mon-Fri, from 1pm Sat & Sun; Ⓜ Green Line to Navy Yard)

Entertainment

Nationals Park
STADIUM

17 ⭐ Map p74, D5

The major-league Washington Nationals play baseball at this spiffy stadium beside the Anacostia River. Don't miss the mid-fourth-inning 'Racing Presidents' – an odd foot race between giant-headed caricatures of past presidents. Hip bars and eateries and playful green spaces surround the ballpark. (☎202-675-6287; www.mlb.com/nationals; 1500 S Capitol St SE; Ⓜ Green Line to Navy Yard)

Rock & Roll Hotel
LIVE MUSIC

18 ⭐ Map p74, G1

The R&R Hotel is a great, grotty spot to catch rockin' live sets from the likes of Thurston Moore and the Dead Kennedys. Don't let the name fool you; this hotel hosts all kinds of music genres from Afrofunk to the city's freshest hip-hop acts, with indie, punk and metal, too. (☎202-388-7625; www. rockandrollhoteldc.com; 1353 H St NE; Ⓜ Red Line to Union Station then streetcar)

Explore

Downtown, Penn Quarter & Logan Circle

This area bustles day and night. Major sights include the National Archives, where the Declaration of Independence is enshrined; the Reynolds Center for American Art & Portraiture, filled with big-name works; and Ford's Theatre, where Abraham Lincoln was assassinated. This is also DC's theater district and convention hub. Trendy bars and restaurants proliferate, especially around Logan Circle.

ANDRIY BLOKHIN/SHUTTERSTOCK ©

The Sights in a Day

☼ Start at the **National Archives** (p84; pictured left), a trove of historical documents including the Declaration of Independence and Constitution. Visit the **Newseum** (p90), a whiz-bang, multistory collection of artifacts and current-events exhibits. Tour **Ford's Theatre** (p90), where John Wilkes Booth shot Abraham Lincoln.

☀ Indulge in a top-end lunch at **Rasika** (p94) or **Central Michel Richard** (p93), or grab a dreamy sandwich at **A Baked Joint** (p93). Spend a few hours browsing the excellent **Reynolds Center for American Art & Portraiture** (p86). The underappreciated **National Building Museum** (p92) and **National Museum of Women in the Arts** (p92) also beckon.

☾ See a theater performance. The **Capitol Steps** (p96) do political shtick. **Shakespeare Theatre Company** (p96) puts on the bard's plays. **Studio Theatre** (p97) and **Woolly Mammoth Theatre Company** (p96) stage contemporary and experimental works. For sustenance stroll up to Logan Circle to **Le Diplomate** (p94) or **Churchkey** (p96), or wander near the Convention Center for the **Dabney** (p92), **Columbia Room** (p95) or **Chercher** (p93).

◉ Top Sights

National Archives (p84)

Reynolds Center for American Art & Portraiture (p86)

♥ Best of Washington, DC

Eating

Dabney (p92)

Chercher (p93)

Shouk (p94)

Theater & Performing Arts

Shakespeare Theatre Company (p96)

Woolly Mammoth Theatre Company (p96)

Studio Theatre (p97)

Ford's Theatre (p90)

Capitol Steps (p96)

Getting There

Ⓜ **Metro** All six Metro lines cross downtown. Main stations include Metro Center (where the Red, Orange, Silver and Blue Lines hub), Gallery Pl-Chinatown (where the Green, Yellow and Red Lines merge) and Mt Vernon Sq/7th St-Convention Center (on the Green, Yellow Lines).

Top Sights
National Archives

You're in line with school group mobs, annoyed, thinking your time might be better spent elsewhere. Then you enter the dim rotunda and see them – the Declaration of Independence, Constitution and Bill of Rights – the USA's founding documents. The Archives has the real, yellowing, spidery-handwriting-scrawled parchments. And your jaw drops. There's John Hancock's signature, and Ben Franklin's and Thomas Jefferson's!

👁 Map p88, C7

www.archives.gov/museum

700 Pennsylvania Ave NW

admission free

🕐 10am-5:30pm

Ⓜ Green, Yellow Lines to Archives

The Declaration of Independence on display

Declaration of Independence

The star documents are laid out in chronological order from left to right in the rotunda. Don't expect to linger over any of them – guards make you keep moving. First up is the Declaration (1776). It's in pretty good shape considering it has moved around so often, including evacuations to Virginia during the War of 1812 and to Fort Knox, KY, during WWII.

Constitution & Bill of Rights

Next up is the Constitution (1787). A clerk named Jacob Shallus set quill to parchment and penned the document's 4543 words in two days. He was paid $30. Editors in the group can try to spot the spelling error (hint: look at the list of signatories, at the word that starts with 'p' and ends with 'sylvania'). The Bill of Rights (1789) unfurls in the next display case.

Public Vaults

After the rotunda, head through the hall to the Public Vaults. Browse George Washington's handwritten letters and Abraham Lincoln's wartime telegrams. There's a nifty piece of paperwork from Charles 'Pa' Ingalls (of *Little House on the Prairie* fame) showing his grant application for 154 acres in the Dakota Territory. You can also watch vintage D-Day reels.

Magna Carta

A 1297 version of the Magna Carta is on view in the Rubenstein Gallery. It inspired America's founding fathers with its assertion of individual rights and protections against a tyrannical ruler. The Constitution's Fifth Amendment is a direct descendant of the older document.

HISHAM IBRAHIM/GETTY IMAGES ©

☑ Top Tips

▶ In spring and summer, reserve tickets in advance on the website for $1.50 each. This lets you go through the fast-track entrance on Constitution Dr (to the right of the steps) versus the general entrance, where queues can be lengthy.

▶ Peruse the Archives Shop for top-notch souvenirs.

▶ To get your bearings: the rotunda and Public Vaults are on the upper level; the Magna Carta and shop are on the ground level (the same as the entrance).

✕ Take a Break

Pop in to **Red Apron Butchery** (☏202-524-5244; www.redapronbutchery.com; 709 D St NW; mains $5-10; ⊙8:30am-8pm Mon-Fri, 9am-8pm Sat, 9am-5pm Sun; Ⓜ Green, Yellow Lines to Archives) for coffee and filling sandwiches made with local, sustainable ingredients.

Indulge in cutting-edge Indian food in modernist environs at Rasika (p94).

Top Sights
Reynolds Center for American Art & Portraiture

If you only visit one art museum in DC, make it the Reynolds Center, which combines the National Portrait Gallery and American Art Museum. There is no better collection of American art in the world than at these two Smithsonian museums. They occupy three floors in the 19th-century US Patent Office building, a neoclassical beauty that hosted Lincoln's second inaugural ball.

Map p88, C6

www.americanart.si.edu

cnr 8th & F Sts NW

admission free

11:30am-7pm

M Red, Yellow, Green Lines to Gallery Pl-Chinatown

O'Keeffe, Hopper & Folk Art

The American Experience gallery (1st floor) hangs blockbusters such as Georgia O'Keeffe's flowery pink *Manhattan* and Edward Hopper's trapped woman in *Cape Cod Morning*. The nearby folk-art gallery holds a vivid collection, especially artwork by African American artists. Look for James Hampton's exquisite, foil-made throne. It's the only piece the artist ever made, a masterwork that took 14 years.

Historic Portraits

The America's Presidents gallery (2nd floor) gives due to 44 heads of state. Gilbert Stuart's rosy-cheeked *George Washington* is the most beloved. The 'cracked plate' photo of Abraham Lincoln is also here. Then seek out *Benjamin Franklin*. You'll recognize the image, as it's the same one that now graces the $100 bill. Ben's portrait enriches the American Origins gallery (1st floor).

Modern Art

Looking for something a little more 20th-century? The 3rd floor has Andy Warhol's pop-art version of Marilyn Monroe and groovy paintings by Roy Lichtenstein, Franz Kline and more modern blue-chip artists. Nam June Paik's neon *Electric Superhighway* will sear your retinas.

Luce Center

The Luce Center, the museum's open storage area, spills across the 3rd and 4th floors. Wander around the trove and ogle cases of paintings. Peruse shelves stacked with sculptures, ceramics and other gorgeous objets d'art. The center has its own information desk that provides free audio tours.

TIM SLOAN/AFP/GETTY IMAGES ©

☑ Top Tips

▶ The Reynolds Center makes a good stop later in the day, given its hours of operation.

▶ Don't overlook the changing exhibitions. The museum curates excellent ones, including shows by big-name artists.

▶ Ask at any of the info desks for the *10 Highlights* brochure.

▶ The museum hosts loads of free public programs, including docent-led tours, concerts, artist talks and sketching classes. Check the daily events calendar online.

✗ Take a Break

The museum's 1st-floor inner courtyard, roofed with slanting glass and dotted with olive trees and marble benches, is a lovely spot. Bring your own picnic or order sandwiches at the cafe (11:30am to 6:30pm; mains $9 to $13).

Matchbox Pizza (p95) beckons nearby with crisp-crust pie and craft brews.

For reviews see

◎ Top Sights   p84
◎ Sights   p90
⊗ Eating   p92
⊗ Drinking   p95
⊗ Entertainment   p96
🛍 Shopping   p97

Sights

Newseum
MUSEUM

1 ◎ Map p88, D7

This six-story, highly interactive news museum is worth the admission price. You can delve into the major events of recent years (the fall of the Berlin Wall, September 11, Hurricane Katrina), and spend hours watching moving film footage and perusing Pulitzer Prize–winning photographs. The concourse level displays FBI artifacts from prominent news stories, such as the Unabomber's cabin and gangster Whitey Bulger's fishing hat. (☑202-292-6100; www.newseum. org; 555 Pennsylvania Ave NW; adult/child $25/15; ◎9am-5pm; Ⓜ Green, Yellow Lines to Archives)

Ford's Theatre
HISTORIC SITE

2 ◎ Map p88, C6

On April 14, 1865, John Wilkes Booth assassinated Abraham Lincoln in his box seat here. Timed-entry tickets let you see the flag-draped site. They also provide entry to the basement museum (displaying Booth's .44-caliber pistol, his muddy boot etc) and to Petersen House (across the street), where Lincoln died. Arrive early (by 8:30am) because tickets do run out. Better yet, reserve online ($3 fee) to ensure admittance. (☑202-347-4833; www.fords.org; 511 10th St NW; admission free; ◎9am-4:30pm; Ⓜ Red, Orange, Silver, Blue Lines to Metro Center)

International Spy Museum
MUSEUM

3 ◎ Map p88, C6

One of DC's most popular museums is flashy, over the top, and probably guilty of overtly glamming up a life of intelligence-gathering. But who cares? You basically want to see Q's lab, and that's what the Spy Museum feels like. Check out James Bond's tricked-out Aston Martin, the KGB's lipstick-concealed pistol and more. Kids go crazy for this spot, but be warned: lines form long and early. Ease the wait somewhat by reserving online (there's a $2 surcharge per ticket). (☑202-393-7798; www.spymus eum.org; 800 F St NW; adult/child $22/15; ◎9am-7pm mid-Apr–mid-Aug, 10am-6pm rest of year; Ⓜ Red, Yellow, Green Lines to Gallery Pl-Chinatown)

Chinatown
AREA

4 ◎ Map p88, D5

DC's dinky Chinatown is anchored on 7th and H Sts NW. It was once a major Asian entrepôt, but today most Asians in the Washington area live in the Maryland or Virginia suburbs. That said, Chinatown is still an intriguing browse. Enter through **Friendship Arch** (7th & H Sts NW), the largest single-span arch in the world. (7th & H Sts NW; Ⓜ Red, Yellow, Green Lines to Gallery Pl-Chinatown)

Understand

Tragedy at Ford's Theatre

A Murderous Plan

In 1865, just days after the Confederate Army surrendered, President Abraham Lincoln was gunned down in cold blood. John Wilkes Booth – Marylander, famous actor and die-hard believer in the Confederate cause – had long harbored ambitions to bring the US leadership to its knees. On April 14, when he stopped by Ford's Theatre to retrieve his mail, he learned the president would be attending a play that evening. Booth decided it was time to strike. He met with his co-conspirators and hatched a plan: Lewis Powell would kill Secretary of State William Seward at his home, while George Atzerodt killed Vice President Andrew Johnson at his residence and Booth struck Lincoln – all would happen simultaneously around 10pm. As it turns out, only Booth would succeed in his mission.

Assassination & Getaway

That night, as Booth strolled up to Lincoln's box, no one questioned him, as he was a well-known actor at Ford's. He crept inside and barricaded the outer door behind him (Lincoln's bodyguard had headed to a nearby pub at intermission and never returned). Booth knew the play well, and waited to act until he heard the funniest line of the play '...you sockdologizing old man-trap!' As the audience predictably erupted in laughter, Booth crept behind Lincoln and shot him in the head.

The president's lifeless body slumped forward. Mary Lincoln screamed and Major Henry Rathbone, also in Lincoln's box, tried to seize the assassin. Booth stabbed him then leaped onto the stage. His foot, however, became entangled in the flag decorating the box, and he landed badly, fracturing his leg. He stumbled to his feet and held the bloody dagger aloft, saying *Sic semper tyrannis!'* ('Thus to all tyrants!'). Booth fled the theater, mounted his waiting horse and galloped off to meet his co-conspirators.

Death Toll

Lincoln never regained consciousness. He was carried across the street to the Petersen House, where he died early the next morning. In a massive manhunt, Booth was hunted down and shot to death less than two weeks later. His alleged co-conspirators were also discovered, brought to trial and executed on July 7.

National Building Museum

MUSEUM

5 Map p88, E6

Devoted to architecture and urban design, the museum is appropriately housed in a magnificent 1887 edifice modeled after the Renaissance-era Palazzo Farnese in Rome. Four stories of ornamented balconies flank the dramatic 316ft-wide atrium, and the Corinthian columns rise 75ft high. There's no charge to view the glimmering public areas; the admission fee is for the exhibits, which will please architecture buffs. (☑202-272-2448; www.nbm.org; 401 F St NW; adult/child $10/7; ☉10am-5pm Mon-Sat, from 11am Sun; ☖; Ⓜ Red Line to Judiciary Sq)

National Museum of Women in the Arts

MUSEUM

6 Map p88, B5

The only US museum exclusively devoted to women's artwork fills this Renaissance Revival mansion. Its collection – 2600 works by almost 700 female artists from 28 countries – moves from Renaissance artists such as Lavinia Fontana to 20th-century works by Frida Kahlo, Georgia O'Keeffe and Helen Frankenthaler. Placards give feminist interpretations of various art movements. It's free the first Sunday of each month. (☑20 2-783-5000; www.nmwa.org; 1250 New York Ave NW; adult/child $10/free; ☉10am-5pm Mon-Sat, from noon Sun; Ⓜ Red, Orange, Silver, Blue Lines to Metro Center)

Touchstone Gallery

GALLERY

7 Map p88, C4

Touchstone Gallery exhibits contemporary pieces created by its 45 member artists. Works cover multiple media, including sculpture, painting and the occasional esoteric installation. The bright, welcoming space always has something eye-popping going on. (☑202-347-2787; www.touchstonegallery.com; 901 New York Ave NW; admission free; ☉11am-6pm Wed-Fri, noon-5pm Sat & Sun; Ⓜ Red, Orange, Silver, Blue Lines to Metro Center)

Eating

Dabney

AMERICAN $$$

8 Map p88, C3

Chef Jeremiah Langhorne studied historic cookbooks, discovering recipes that used local ingredients and lesser-explored flavors in his quest to resuscitate mid-Atlantic cuisine lost to the ages. Most of the dishes are even cooked over a wood-burning hearth. But this isn't George Washington's resto. Chef Langhorne has given it all

Top Tip

News Source

Want to know what's happening back home? Stroll up to the Newseum (p90), where front pages of newspapers from around the world – as well as from every US state – are displayed daily by the entrance.

a modern twist – enough to earn him a Michelin star. (📞202-450-1015; www.thedabney.com; 122 Blagden Alley NW; small plates $14-22; ⏰5:30-10pm Tue-Thu, 5:30-11pm Fri & Sat, 5-10pm Sun; Ⓜ Green, Yellow Line to Mount Vernon Square/7th St-Convention Center)

A Baked Joint
CAFE $

9 Map p88, E4

Order at the counter then take your luscious, heaped-on-housemade-bread sandwich – perhaps the roasted sweet potato and goat cheese on focaccia, or the Nutella and banana on whole-wheat sourdough – to a bench or table in the big, open room. Natural light streams in the floor-to-ceiling windows. Not hungry? It's also a great place for a well-made latte. (📞202-408-6985; www.abakedjoint.com; 440 K St NW; mains $5-11; ⏰7am-8pm Mon-Thu, 7am-9pm Fri, 8am-8pm Sat & Sun; Ⓜ Red, Yellow, Green Lines to Gallery Pl-Chinatown)

Central Michel Richard
AMERICAN $$$

10 Map p88, B7

Michel Richard was one of Washington's first star chefs. He died in 2016, but his namesake Central blazes onward. It's a special dining experience, eating in a four-star bistro where the food is old-school, comfort-food favorites with a twist: perhaps lobster burgers, or a sinfully complex meatloaf, or fried chicken that redefines what fried chicken can be. (📞202-626-0015; www.centralmichelrichard.com; 1001 Pennsylvania Ave NW; mains $25-35;

Central Michel Richard

⏰11:30am-2:30pm Mon-Fri, 5-10pm Mon-Thu, 5-10:30pm Fri & Sat, 11am-2:30pm Sun; Ⓜ Orange, Silver, Blue Lines to Federal Triangle)

Chercher
ETHIOPIAN $

11 Map p88, C2

Ethiopian expats have been known to compare Chercher's food to their grandma's home cooking. It prepares terrific *injera* (spongy bread) for dipping into hot spiced *wats* (stews). Vegetarians will find lots to devour. There's beer and honey wine from the motherland, and spices you can buy. The restaurant spreads over two floors in an intimate townhouse with brightly painted walls and artwork. (📞202-299-9703; www.chercherrestaurant.com; 1334 9th St NW; mains $11-17; ⏰11am-

⊙ Local Life

El Sol

El Sol (☎202-815-4789; www.elsol-dc.com; 1227 11th St NW; tacos $2.50-3, mains $10-16; ⊙10am-1am Sun-Thu, to 2am Fri & Sat; Ⓜ Green, Yellow Lines to Mt Vernon Sq/7th St-Convention Center) feels like a sunny neighborhood taqueria, but the food goes way beyond. Thin, crisp corn tortillas cradle juicy chicken, slow-braised pork, cactus paddles and other fillings, with almost all ingredients made in house (the mole sauce comes from the chef's mom in Mexico).

11pm Mon-Sat, noon-10pm Sun; ☝; Ⓜ Green, Yellow Lines to Mt Vernon Sq/7th St-Convention Center)

Rasika   INDIAN $$

12 ✗ Map p88, D7

Rasika is as cutting-edge as Indian food gets. The room resembles a Jaipur palace decorated by a flock of modernist art-gallery curators. Top marks go to the *murgh mussalam*, a plate of juicy tandoori chicken with cashews and quail eggs; and to the deceptively simple *dal* (lentils), which have just the right kiss of sharp fenugreek. Vegetarians will feel a lot of love here. (☎202-637-1222; www.rasikarestaurant.com; 633 D St NW; mains $14-28; ⊙11:30am-2:30pm Mon-Fri, 5:30-10:30pm Mon-Thu, 5-11pm Fri & Sat; ☝; Ⓜ Green, Yellow Lines to Archives)

Le Diplomate   FRENCH $$$

13 ✗ Map p88, A1

This charming French bistro is one of the hottest tables in town. DC celebrities galore cozy up in the leather banquettes and at the sidewalk tables. They come for an authentic slice of Paris, from the *coq au vin* (wine-braised chicken) and aromatic baguettes to the vintage curios and nudie photos decorating the bathrooms. Make reservations. (☎202-332-3333; www.lediplomatedc.com; 1601 14th St NW; mains $23-35; ⊙5-11pm Mon-Thu, 5pm-midnight Fri, 9:30am-midnight Sat, 9:30am-11pm Sun; Ⓜ Green, Yellow Lines to U St)

Shouk   ISRAELI $

14 ✗ Map p88, D4

Small, fast-casual Shouk creates big flavor in its vegan menu of Israeli street food. A crazy-good burger made of chickpeas, black beans, lentils and mushrooms gets stuffed into a toasty pita with pickled turnips, arugula and charred onions. The mushroom-and-cauliflower pita and sweet-potato fries with cashew *labneh* (creamy 'cheese') are other lip smackers. Craft beer and tap wine add to the pleasure. (☎202-652-1464; www.shouk.com; 655 K St NW; mains $10; ⊙11am-10pm; ☝; Ⓜ Green, Yellow Lines to Mt Vernon Sq/7th St-Convention Center)

Zaytinya

MEDITERRANEAN **$$**

15 Map p88, C5

One of the culinary crown jewels of chef José Andrés, ever-popular Zaytinya serves superb Greek, Turkish and Lebanese mezze (small plates) in a long, noisy dining room with soaring ceilings and all-glass walls. It's a favorite after-work meet-up spot. (☏202-638-0800; www.zaytinya.com; 701 9th St NW; mezze $8-14; ◷11am-10pm Sun & Mon, to 11pm Tue-Thu, to midnight Fri & Sat; ◢; Ⓜ Red, Yellow, Green Lines to Gallery Pl-Chinatown)

Matchbox Pizza

PIZZA **$$**

16 Map p88, D5

The pizza here has a devout following of gastronomes and the restaurant's warm, exposed-brick interior typically is packed. What's so good about it? Fresh ingredients, a thin, blistered crust baked by angels, and more fresh ingredients. Oh, and the beer list rocks, with Belgian ales and hopped-up craft brews flowing from the taps. Reserve ahead to avoid a wait. (☏202-289-4441; www.matchboxrestaurants.com; 713 H St NW; 10in pizzas $13-15; ◷11am-10:30pm Mon-Thu, 11am-11:30pm Fri, 10am-11:30pm Sat, 10am-10:30pm Sun; Ⓜ Red, Yellow, Green Lines to Gallery Pl-Chinatown)

Drinking

Columbia Room

COCKTAIL BAR

17 Map p88, C2

Serious mixology goes on at Columbia Room, the kind of place that sources spring water from Kentucky to Scotland, and uses pickled cherry blossom and barley tea among its ingredients. But it's done in a refreshingly non-snooty environment. Choose from three distinct areas: the festive Punch Garden on the outdoor roof deck, the comfy, leather-chair-dotted Spirits Library, or the 14-seat, prix-fixe Tasting Room. (☏202-316-9396; www.columbiaroomdc.com; 124 Blagden Alley NW; ◷5pm-12:30am Tue-Thu, to 1:30am Fri & Sat; Ⓜ Green, Yellow Lines to Mt Vernon Sq/7th St-Convention Center)

Dacha Beer Garden

BEER GARDEN

18 Map p88, D1

Happiness reigns in Dacha's freewheeling beer garden. Kids and dogs bound around the picnic tables, while adults hoist glass boots filled with German brews. When the weather gets nippy, staff bring heaters and blankets and stoke the fire pit. And it all takes place under the sultry gaze of Elizabeth Taylor (or a mural of her, which sprawls across the back wall). (☏202-350-9888; www.dachadc.com; 1600 7th St NW; ◷4-10:30pm Mon-Thu, noon-midnight Fri & Sat, 11am-10:30pm Sun; Ⓜ Green, Yellow Lines to Shaw-Howard U)

Top Tip

Pre-Theater Menus

Many restaurants in the neighborhood offer pre-theater menus. This generally means a three-course meal for around $37.50, offered before 6:30pm. Rasika (p94) and Central Michel Richard (p93) are among those that offer such deals.

Churchkey
BAR

19 Map p88, A2

Coppery, mod-industrial Churchkey glows with hipness. Fifty beers flow from the taps, including five brain-walloping, cask-aged ales. If none of those please you, another 500 types of brew are available by bottle (including gluten-free suds). Churchkey is the upstairs counterpart to **Birch & Barley** (www.birchandbarley.com; mains $16-29; ⏱5:30-10pm Tue-Thu, 5:30-11pm Fri & Sat, 11am-8pm Sun), a popular nouveau comfort-food restaurant, and you can order much of its menu at the bar. (☎202-567-2576; www.churchkeydc.com; 1337 14th St NW; ⏱4pm-1am Mon-Thu, 4pm-2am Fri, 11:30am-2am Sat, 11:30am-1am Sun; Ⓜ Orange, Silver, Blue Lines to McPherson Sq)

Entertainment

Shakespeare Theatre Company
THEATER

20 ⭐ Map p88, D6

The nation's foremost Shakespeare company presents masterful works by the bard, as well as plays by George Bernard Shaw, Oscar Wilde, Eugene O'Neill and other greats. The season spans about a half-dozen productions annually, plus a free summer Shakespeare series on-site for two weeks in late August. (☎202-547-1122; www.shakespearetheatre.org; 450 7th St NW; Ⓜ Green, Yellow Lines to Archives)

Woolly Mammoth Theatre Company
THEATER

21 ⭐ Map p88, D7

Woolly Mammoth is the edgiest of DC's experimental groups. For most shows, $20 'stampede' seats are available at the box office two hours before performances. They're limited in number, and sold first-come, first-served, so get there early. (☎202-393-3939; www.woollymammoth.net; 641 D St NW; Ⓜ Green, Yellow Lines to Archives)

Capitol Steps
COMEDY

22 ⭐ Map p88, A7

This singing troupe claims to be the only group in America that tries to be funnier than Congress. It's composed of current and former congressional staffers, so they know their political stuff, although sometimes it can be overtly corny. The satirical, bipartisan jokes poke fun at both sides of the spectrum. (☎202-397-7328; www.capsteps.com; Ronald Reagan Bldg, 1300 Pennsylvania Ave NW; tickets $40.50; ⏱shows 7:30pm Fri & Sat; Ⓜ Orange, Silver, Blue Lines to Federal Triangle)

Studio Theatre

THEATER

23 ⭐ Map p88, A1

This contemporary four-theater complex has been staging Pulitzer Prize–winning and premiere plays for more than 35 years. It cultivates a lot of local actors. (☏202-332-3300; www.studiotheatre.org; 1501 14th St NW; Ⓜ Red Line to Dupont Circle)

National Theatre

THEATER

24 ⭐ Map p88, B6

Washington's oldest continuously operating theater shows flashy Broadway musicals and big-name productions. A lottery for $25 tickets (cash only) takes place two hours prior to every show; submit your name at the box office. Saturday mornings feature free performances for children at 9:30am and 11am. (☏202-628-6161; www.thenationaldc.org; 1321 Pennsylvania Ave NW; Ⓜ Red, Orange, Silver, Blue Lines to Metro Center)

Verizon Center

STADIUM

25 ⭐ Map p88, D6

The ever-busy facility is DC's arena for big-name concerts and sporting events. Washington's rough-and-tumble pro hockey team the Capitals (www.nhl.com/capitals) and pro basketball team the Wizards (www.nba.com/wizards) both play here from October through April. Tickets start from around $40. (☏202-628-3200; www.monumentalsportsnetwork.com/events; 601 F St NW; Ⓜ Red, Yellow, Green Lines to Gallery Pl-Chinatown)

RITU MANOJ JETHANI/SHUTTERSTOCK ©

CityCenterDC

Shopping

CityCenterDC

SHOPPING CENTER

26 🔒 Map p88, C5

Rodeo Drive chic may not be the first way you'd think of describing Washington, but this sparkling, open-air oasis of shops and eateries blows that notion straight out of your Dior flacon. Style mavens poke into high-end boutiques. Diners indulge in haute cuisine. And the best part? The fountain-splashed courtyard tucked away from downtown bustle; order an espresso and relax awhile. (☏202-289-9000; www.citycenterdc.com; H St NW, between 9th St NW &11th St NW; Ⓜ Red, Orange, Silver, Blue Lines to Metro Center; Red, Yellow, Green Lines to Gallery Pl-Chinatown)

Explore

Dupont Circle

Dupont offers flashy new restaurants, hip bars, cafe society and cool bookstores. The neighborhood has Washington's highest concentration of embassies, many set in historic mansions. It's also the heart of the LGBT community. A few overlooked museums are here, but mostly Dupont is about wandering around and soaking up the urban-cool vibe.

ANDREI MEDVEDEV/SHUTTERSTOCK ©

The Sights in a Day

 Energize for the day ahead with coffee and pastries at **Un Je Ne Sais Quoi** (p106). Get cultured in under-the-radar museums: the **Phillips Collection** (p104) offers Renoirs and other modern art, while the **National Geographic Society Museum** (p104) often has intriguing exhibits in its worldly galleries.

 Grab an epicurean sandwich at **Bub & Pop's** (p105) or a casual meal at **Zorba's Cafe** (p106). It'll be good fuel for a mosey along eye-popping **Embassy Row** (p104). Afterward poke around **Second Story Books** (p109) and **Tabletop** (p109), then hit happy hour at **St Arnold's Mussel Bar** (p106) or **Bier Baron** (p108).

 Have dinner in one of the sublime restaurants. Get in line at **Little Serow** (p104), or hopefully you reserved at **Obelisk** (p105) or **Blue Duck Tavern** (p107). As the night rolls on, take advantage of Dupont's active nightlife scene. Shake a tail with the beautiful people under the chandeliers at **18th Street Lounge** (p107) or at a wild dance party at **Cobalt** (p108). Those looking for a more relaxed vibe can sip cocktails at **Bar Charley** (p107).

For a local's day in Dupont Circle, see p100.

Local Life

A Night Out in Dupont Circle (p100)

♥ Best of Washington, DC

Eating
Bistrot du Coin (p100)

Un Je Ne Sais Quoi (p106)

Bars & Clubs
Bar Charley (p107)

18th Street Lounge (p107)

Board Room (p101)

Gay & Lesbian
JR's (p101)

Larry's Lounge (p107)

Cobalt (p108)

Kramerbooks (p101)

Getting There

Ⓜ **Metro** Dupont Circle (Red Line) for most points. Use the Q St exit for destinations north of P St, and the 19th St exit for destinations south. Farragut North (Red Line) is closer to M St.

🚌 **Bus** Catch the DC Circulator's Dupont–Georgetown–Rosslyn bus at 19th and N Sts (use the south exit from Dupont Metro station).

Local Life
A Night Out in Dupont Circle

Dupont gets busy once the sun goes down. Young professionals of all stripes and persuasions gather with friends to drink, dine and sing karaoke. They play board games, quaff sparkling wines, indulge in late-night gelato and curries, and flirt with each other in the 3am bookshop on weekends.

1 Wine at Bistro du Coin

Lively and much-loved **Bistrot du Coin** (📞202-234-6969; www.bistrotducoin. com; 1738 Connecticut Ave NW; mains $16-29; ⏱11:30am-midnight Mon-Wed, 11:30am-1am Thu & Fri, noon-1am Sat, noon-midnight Sun; MRed Line to Dupont Circle) is a neighborhood favorite for roll-up-your sleeves, working-class French fare. If it's busy, try for a bar seat. Wines from around the motherland can be gulped by the glass, carafe and bottle.

❷ Board Room's Games

Grab a beer, settle in at a table and crush your opponent at Hungry Hungry Hippos. Or summon spirits with a ouija board. **Board Room** (☏ 202-518-7666; www.boardroomdc.com; 1737 Connecticut Ave NW; ⏱ 4pm-2am Mon-Thu, 4pm-3am Fri, noon-3am Sat, noon-2am Sun; Ⓜ Red Line to Dupont Circle) lets you flash back to childhood via stacks of board games. Battleship, Risk, Operation – name it, and it's here to rent for $2.

❸ Gelato at Dolcezza

Dolcezza (☏ 202-299-9116; www.dolcezzagelato.com; 1704 Connecticut Ave NW; gelato $5-8; ⏱ 7am-10pm Mon-Thu, 7am-11pm Fri, 8am-11pm Sat, 8am-10pm Sun; Ⓜ Red Line to Dupont Circle) scoops a dozen or so creamy flavors of gelato. They're not your everyday spoonful, with varieties such as strawberry tarragon. Don't be timid – they're divine.

❹ Late-Night Books

Open almost round the clock on weekends, **Kramerbooks** (☏ 202-387-1400; www.kramers.com; 1517 Connecticut Ave NW; ⏱ 7:30am-1am Sun-Thu, to 3am Fri & Sat; Ⓜ Red Line to Dupont Circle) – along with its attached Afterwords Cafe and bar – is as much a spot for schmoozing as for shopping. Grab a meal, have a pint and flirt with strangers (the store is a fabled pick-up spot for straights and gays).

❺ Underground Art

An enormous, abandoned streetcar station lies beneath Dupont Circle, and a local arts group has transformed it into **Dupont Underground** (www.dupont underground.org; 1583 New Hampshire Ave NW; $15; Ⓜ Red Line to Dupont Circle), a cool gallery of art, architecture and design. Check online for exhibition times.

❻ Curry at Duke's Grocery

Duke's Grocery (☏ 202-733-5623; www.dukesgrocery.com; 1513 17th St NW; mains $12-16; ⏱ 11am-10pm Mon & Tue, 11am-1am Wed & Thu, 11am-2am Fri, 10am-2am Sat, 10am-10pm Sun; Ⓜ Red Line to Dupont Circle) takes its cue from East London's corner cafes and curry houses. Runny eggs and toast for breakfast, lamb *kofta* (meatballs) for dinner – a chalkboard lists the daily-changing menu. The convivial tables spread over two floors amid mismatched armchairs and vintage photos.

❼ Karaoke at JR's

Gay hangout **JR's** (☏ 202-328-0090; www.jrsbar-dc.com; 1519 17th St NW; ⏱ 4pm-2am Mon-Thu, 4pm-3am Fri, 1pm-3am Sat, 1pm-2am Sun; Ⓜ Red Line to Dupont Circle) is usually packed. While it's mostly guys aged under 40 in natty-casual attire who are chatting over their beers, the dark-wood and stained-glass bar is welcoming to all. Show-tunes karaoke is great fun on Monday nights.

❽ Tabard Inn Cocktails

The **Tabard Inn Bar** (☏ 202-331-8528; www.tabardinn.com; 1739 N St NW; ⏱ 4pm-11pm; Ⓜ Red Line to Dupont Circle) is in a hotel, but plenty of locals come to swirl an old-fashioned or gin and tonic in the wood-beamed, lodge-like lounge. On warm nights, maneuver for an outdoor table on the ivy-clad patio.

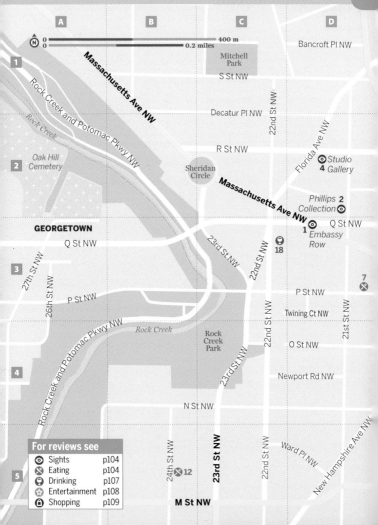

N 0 ————— 400 m
0 ————— 0.2 miles

Bancroft Pl NW

Massachusetts Ave NW

Mitchell Park

S St NW

Decatur Pl NW

22nd St NW

R St NW

Florida Ave NW

Oak Hill Cemetery

Sheridan Circle

Massachusetts Ave NW

Rock Creek and Potomac Pkwy NW

Rock Creek

Studio 4 **Gallery**

Phillips 2 Collection

Q St NW 1 *Embassy Row*

GEORGETOWN

Q St NW

23rd St NW

22nd St NW

18

7

P St NW

27th St NW

26th St NW

P St NW

Twining Ct NW

21st St NW

Rock Creek

Rock Creek Park

22nd St NW

O St NW

23rd St NW

Rock Creek and Potomac Pkwy NW

Newport Rd NW

N St NW

22nd St NW

Ward Pl NW

New Hampshire Ave NW

24th St NW

12

23rd St NW

M St NW

For reviews see	
⊙ Sights	p104
⊗ Eating	p104
⊖ Drinking	p107
⊙ Entertainment	p108
⊙ Shopping	p109

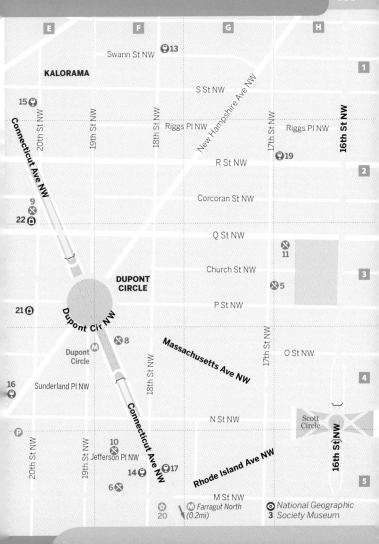

Sights

Embassy Row
ARCHITECTURE

1 Map p102, D3

Want to take a trip around the world? Stroll northwest along Massachusetts Ave from Dupont Circle (the actual traffic circle) and you pass more than 40 embassies housed in mansions that range from elegant to discreet. Tunisia, Chile, Haiti – flags flutter above heavy doors and mark the nations inside, while dark-windowed sedans ease out of driveways ferrying diplomats to and fro. The district has another 130 embassies sprinkled throughout, but this is the main vein. (www.embassy.org; Massachusetts Ave NW btwn Observatory & Dupont Circles NW; ⓂRed Line to Dupont Circle)

Phillips Collection
MUSEUM

2 Map p102, D2

The first modern-art museum in the country (opened in 1921) houses an exquisite collection of European and American works. Renoir's *Luncheon of the Boating Party* is a highlight, along with pieces by Gauguin, Van Gogh, Picasso and many other greats. The intimate rooms put you unusually close to the artworks. The permanent collection is free on weekdays. Download the free app or dial 𝄞202-595-1839 for audio tours through the works. (𝄞202-387-2151; www.phillipscollection.org; 1600 21st St NW; Tue-Fri free, Sat & Sun $10, ticketed exhibitions per day $12; ⓒ10am-5pm Tue, Wed, Fri & Sat, to 8:30pm Thu, noon-7pm Sun; ⓂRed Line to Dupont Circle)

National Geographic Society Museum
MUSEUM

3 Map p102, G5

The museum at National Geographic Society headquarters can't compete with the Smithsonian's more extensive offerings, but it can be worth a stop, depending on what's showing. Exhibits are drawn from the society's well-documented expeditions to the far corners of the Earth, and they change every three months or so. (𝄞202-857-7700; www.nationalgeographic.org/dc; 1145 17th St NW; adult/child $15/10; ⓒ10am-6pm; ⓂRed Line to Farragut North)

Studio Gallery
GALLERY

4 Map p102, D2

Studio Gallery shows contemporary works by more than 35 emerging DC-area artists. Paintings, sculpture, mixed media and video are represented. The relatively small space spans the main floor and basement, with exhibits that always feel fresh. Openings are held on the first Friday of the month. (𝄞202-232-8734; www.studiogallerydc.com; 2108 R St NW; admission free; ⓒ1-6pm Wed-Fri, 11am-6pm Sat; ⓂRed Line to Dupont Circle)

Eating

Little Serow
THAI $$$

5 Map p102, H3

Little Serow has no phone, no reservations and no sign on the door. It only seats groups of four or fewer (larger parties will be separated),

Croatian Embassy (p129), Embassy Row

but despite all this, people line up around the block. And what for? Superlative Northern Thai cuisine. The single-option menu – which consists of six or so hot-spiced courses – changes by the week. (www. littleserow.com; 1511 17th St NW; set menu $49; ◷5:30-10pm Tue-Thu, to 10:30pm Fri & Sat; Ⓜ Red Line to Dupont Circle)

Bub & Pop's
SANDWICHES $

 6 ◍ Map p102, F5

A chef tired of the fine-dining rat race opened this gourmet sandwich shop with his parents. Ingredients are made from scratch in house – the meatballs, pickles, mayonnaise, roasted pork. Congenial mom Arlene rules

the counter and can answer questions about any of it. The sandwiches are enormous, and best consumed hot off the press in the bright aqua and red room. (☏202-457-1111; www.bubandpops. com; 1815 M St NW; sandwiches half/whole $10/18; ◷11am-4pm Mon-Sat; Ⓜ Red Line to Dupont Circle)

Obelisk
ITALIAN $$$

7 ◍ Map p102, D3

Obelisk's small and narrow dining room feels almost like eating at someone's kitchen table. The set-course Italian feasts are prepared with first-rate ingredients. You might sup on ricotta ravioli with green tomato sauce, or braised duck leg with pear sauce; the antipasti in particular is a revelation. The menu changes daily but doesn't give you much selection (picky eaters should call ahead). Make reservations. (☏202-872-1180; www.obeliskdc.com; 2029 P St NW; 5-course menu $78-88; ◷6-10pm Tue-Sat; Ⓜ Red Line to Dupont Circle)

Un Je Ne Sais Quoi

BAKERY $

8 Map p102, F4

The smell of rich coffee envelopes you when you enter this little bakery, where a couple of French expats bake *merveilleux*, their signature pastry plumped with layers of meringue and ganache. It's like biting into a glorious cloud. Tarts, eclairs and other sweets are equally exquisite, served on china plates amid beautiful vintage Parisian decor. (☏202-721-0099; www.facebook.com/unjenesaisquoi pastry; 1361 Connecticut Ave NW; pastries $2.50-5; ◷7:30am-7:30pm Mon-Thu, to 8pm Fri, 10am-8pm Sat; Ⓜ Red Line to Dupont Circle)

◯ Local Life
Dupont Circle Market

The **Dupont Circle Market** (www.freshfarmmarkets.org; 1500 20th St NW; ◷8:30am-1:30pm Sun Apr-Dec, 10am-1pm Jan-Mar; Ⓜ Red Line to Dupont Circle) teems with locals on Sunday morning. It's part of the Fresh Farm Market program, one of the leaders of the Chesapeake Bay region local-food movement.

Zorba's Cafe

GREEK $

9 Map p102, E2

Generous portions of moussaka and souvlaki, as well as pitchers of Rolling Rock beer, make family-run Zorba's Cafe one of DC's best bargain haunts. On warm days the outdoor patio packs with locals. With the bouzouki music playing in the background, you can almost imagine you're in the Greek islands. (☏202-387-8555; www.zorbascafe.com; 1612 20th St NW; mains $13-16; ◷11am-11:30pm Mon-Sat, to 10:30pm Sun; Ⓜ Red Line to Dupont Circle)

St Arnold's Mussel Bar

BELGIAN $$

10 Map p102, F5

Mussels and *frites* (fries) hit the tables in innumerable varieties: in Thai curry sauce, bleu cheese and bacon sauce, and the house specialty beer sauce with caramelized shallots and duck fat, to name a few. Add the terrific Belgian beers on tap and the warm, convivial ambience, and it's easy to settle in for a while. (☏202-833-1321; www.starnoldsmusselbar.com; 1827 Jefferson Pl NW; mains $14-20; ◷11am-2am Sun-Thu, to 3am Fri & Sat; Ⓜ Red Line to Farragut North)

Hank's Oyster Bar

SEAFOOD $$$

11 Map p102, H3

DC has several oyster bars, but mini-chain Hank's is our favorite, mixing power-player muscle with good-old-boy ambience. As you'd expect, the oyster menu is extensive and excellent; there are always at least four varieties on hand. Quarters are cramped, and you often have to wait for a table – nothing a sake oyster bomb won't fix. (☎202-462 4265; www.hanksoysterbar.com; 1624 Q St NW; mains $22-30; ⏱11:30am-1am Mon & Tue, 11:30am-2am Wed-Fri, 11am-2am Sat, 11am-1am Sun; ⓜRed Line to Dupont Circle)

Blue Duck Tavern

AMERICAN $$$

12 Map p102, B5

The Michelin-starred Blue Duck creates a rustic kitchen ambience in the midst of an uber-urbanized concrete corridor of M St. The changing menu draws from farms across the country, mixing mains such as venison tartare and suckling pig sourced from Pennsylvania, crab cakes from nearby Chesapeake Bay and grits from South Carolina. (☎202-419-6755; www.blueducktavern.com; 1201 24th St NW; mains $29-38; ⏱6:30am-2:30pm & 5:30-10:30pm Sun-Thu, to 11pm Fri & Sat; ☑; ⓜRed Line to Dupont Circle)

Drinking

Bar Charley

BAR

13 Map p102, F1

Bar Charley draws a mixed crowd from the neighborhood – young, old, gay and straight. They come for groovy cocktails sloshing in vintage glassware and ceramic tiki mugs, served at very reasonable prices by DC standards. Try the gin and gingery Suffering Bastard. The beer list isn't huge, but it is thoughtfully chosen

with some wild ales. Around 60 wines are available, too. (☎202-627-2183; www.barcharley.com; 1825 18th St NW; ⏱5pm-12:30am Mon-Thu, 4pm-1:30am Fri, 10am-1:30am Sat, 10am-12:30am Sun; ⓜRed Line to Dupont Circle)

18th Street Lounge

CLUB

14 Map p102, F5

Chandeliers, velvet sofas, antique wallpaper and a ridiculously good-looking, dance-loving crowd adorn this multi-floored mansion. The DJs – spinning funk, soul and Brazilian beats – are phenomenal, which is not surprising given Eric Hilton (of Thievery Corporation) is co-owner. The lack of a sign on the door proclaims the club's exclusivity. No denim or sneakers. Covers range from $10 to $20. (☎202-466-3922; www.eighteenthstreetlounge.com; 1212 18th St NW; ⏱5pm-2am Tue-Thu, 5pm-3am Fri, 9pm-3am Sat, 9pm-2am Sun; ⓜRed Line to Dupont Circle)

Filter

CAFE

15 Map p102, E1

Set on a quiet street, Filter is a jewel-box-sized cafe with a tiny front patio, a hipsterish crowd and, most importantly, great, locally roasted coffee. Those who seek caffeinated perfection can get a decent flat white here. (📞20 2-234-5837; www.filtercoffeehouse.com; 1726 20th St NW; ⊘7am-7pm Mon-Fri, 8am-7pm Sat & Sun; Ⓜ Red Line to Dupont Circle)

Firefly Bar

BAR

16 Map p102, E4

Firefly is a restaurant first – the Hotel Madera's restaurant, to be precise – but we're not listing it for those merits. We can say it's one of the coolest bars in Dupont, decked out with its surreal, magically happy 'firefly trees,' all candlelit and reminiscent of childhood summer evenings, and romantic as hell to boot. The cocktail menu is a glorious thing. (📞202-861-1310; www. firefly-dc.com; 1310 New Hampshire Ave NW; ⊘4-11pm; Ⓜ Red Line to Dupont Circle)

Decades

CLUB

17 Map p102, F5

Decades is a big, booming club with three levels of let-loose dance music. It's good fun, decorated with glowy retro decor and arcade games. No sneakers or athletic gear allowed. (📞202-853-3498; www.decadesdc.com; 1219 Connecticut Ave NW; ⊘6pm-2am Wed, 10pm-2am Thu, 10pm-3am Fri, 9pm-3am Sun; Ⓜ Red Line to Dupont Circle)

Bier Baron

BAR

18 Map p102, C3

Enter the Bier Baron's underground lair and prepare your liver for an onslaught of brews. The dark, dingy, pubby bar taps 50 different beers – emphasis on local and unusual craft suds – and offers 500 more bottled beers from around the world. Aim for a corner seat, order a sampler and settle in for an impressive taste tour. (📞202-293-1887; http://inlovewithbier.com/wordpress2; 1523 22nd St NW; ⊘4pm-midnight Mon-Thu, 4pm-2am Fri, 3pm-2am Sat, 3pm-midnight Sun; Ⓜ Red Line to Dupont Circle)

Cobalt

GAY

19 Map p102, H2

Featuring lots of hair product and buff gym bodies, Cobalt tends to gather a well-dressed late-20s to 30-something crowd who come for fun (but loud!) dance parties throughout the week. The time-hallowed dance club is on the 3rd floor; the venue also has a restaurant on the 1st floor and a lounge on the 2nd. (📞20 2-232-4416; www.cobaltdc.com; 1639 R St NW; ⊘4pm-2am Sun-Thu, to 3am Fri & Sat; Ⓜ Red Line to Dupont Circle)

Entertainment

DC Improv

COMEDY

20 Map p102, F5

DC Improv is comedy in the more traditional sense, featuring stand-up by comics from Comedy Central, Saturday

THE WASHINGTON POST/GETTY IMAGES ©

Dupont Circle Market (p106)

Night Live and HBO in its main theater. The smaller 'lounge showroom' hosts up-and-coming improv troupes, usually with cheaper ticket prices. The venue also offers workshops. (202-296-7008; www.dcimprov.com; 1140 Connecticut Ave NW; tickets from $10; ⊘closed Mon; Ⓜ Red Line to Farragut North)

Shopping

Second Story Books   BOOKS, MUSIC

21 🔒 Map p102, E3

Packed with dusty secondhand tomes, atmospheric Second Story also sells used CDs, antiquarian books and old sheet music. The prices are decent

and the choices are broad. Be sure to browse the sidewalk bins, which have books from 50¢ to $2. (202-659-8884; www.secondstorybooks.com; 2000 P St NW; ⊘10am-10pm; Ⓜ Red Line to Dupont Circle)

Tabletop   HOMEWARES

22 🔒 Map p102, E2

Also known as the best little design store in Dupont, Tabletop is evidence that DC is a lot more stylish than some give it credit for. The whimsical candles, postmodern wine carafes and vintage table linens are sure to impress your artsy and creative friends. (202-387-7117; www.tabletopdc.com; 1608 20th St NW; ⊘noon-8pm Mon-Sat, 10am-6pm Sun; Ⓜ Red Line to Dupont Circle)

Local Life
Exploring Jazzy U Street & Shaw

Getting There

M Green or Yellow Line to U St (for places around U St and 13th St NW) and Shaw-Howard U (for places around T St and 7th St NW).

In the early 1900s, U St was one of the most vibrant African American districts in the country. Duke Ellington was born here and cut his chops in local clubs. Today U St and Shaw (the surrounding area) are DC's 'it' spot. Poetry slams, soul food and, of course, Duke's old jazz hangouts make it a sweet slice of DC life.

1 Open Mike at Busboys & Poets

Busboys & Poets (📞202-387-7638; www.busboysandpoets.com; 2021 14th St NW; mains $11-21; ⏰8am-midnight Mon-Thu, 8am-2am Fri, from 9am Sat & Sun) is one of U St's linchpins. Locals gather for coffee, wi-fi and a progressive vibe (and attached bookstore) that make San Francisco feel conservative. The big event is the open-mike poetry reading every Tuesday from 9pm to 11pm.

2 Half-Smokes at Ben's Chili Bowl

Despite visits by presidents, movie stars and busloads of tourists, **Ben's Chili Bowl** (📞202-667-0909; www.benschilibowl.com; 1213 U St; mains $6-10; ⏰6am-2am Mon-Thu, 6am-4am Fri, 7am-4am Sat, 11am-midnight Sun) remains a real neighborhood spot, with locals downing half-smokes (a meatier, smokier version of the hotdog, usually slathered in the namesake chili) and gossiping over sweet iced tea.

3 Tunes at U Street Music Hall

Two local DJs own and operate **U Street Music Hall** (📞202-588-1889; www.ustreetmusichall.com; 1115 U St NW; ⏰hours vary). It looks like a no-frills rock bar, but it has a pro sound system, cork-cushioned dance floor and other accoutrements of a serious dance club. Alternative bands also thrash a couple of nights per week.

4 Soul Food at Oohh's & Aahh's

Un-notch the belt: the cornbread, collard greens, meatloaf and other soulfood dishes at **Oohh's & Aahh's** (📞202-667-7142; www.oohhsnaahhs.com; 1005 U St NW; mains $14-22; ⏰noon-10pm Mon-Thu, to 4am Fri & Sat, to 7pm Sun) come in enormous portions. Not that hungry? Stop in for a piece of hummingbird (banana-pineapple) cake. Sit at the counter and immerse in the before-U-St-became-gentrified crowd.

5 Art at Foundry Gallery

A nonprofit member-run organization, **Foundry Gallery** (📞202-232-0203; www.foundrygallery.org; 2118 8th St NW; admission free; ⏰1-7pm Wed-Sun) features a diverse range of super-contemporary and local art. Peek in the big, street-level windows to see what's showing. Openings are held on various Saturdays.

6 Beer at Right Proper

As if the artwork – a chalked mural of the National Zoo's giant pandas with laser eyes destroying downtown DC – wasn't enough, **Right Proper Brewing Co** (📞202-607-2337; www.rightproperbrewery.com; 624 T St NW; ⏰5pm-midnight Mon-Thu, 11:30am-1am Fri & Sat, 11:30am-11pm Sun) makes sublime ales in a building where Duke Ellington used to play pool. The brewery is Shaw's happy place.

7 Big Names at Howard Theatre

Built in 1910, **Howard Theatre** (📞202-803-2899; www.thehowardtheatre.com; 620 T St NW) was the top address when U St was known as 'Black Broadway.' Ellington, Ella Fitzgerald, Billie Holiday and other famed names lit the marquee. Now big-name comedians, blues and jazz acts fill the house.

Explore

Adams Morgan

Adams Morgan has long been Washington's fun, nightlife-driven neighborhood. It's also a global village of sorts. The result today is a raucous mash-up centered on 18th St NW. Vintage boutiques, record shops and ethnic eats poke up between thumping bars and a growing number of stylish spots for gastronomes.

The Sights in a Day

☀ Spend a relaxing morning reading, drinking coffee and fueling up on omelets and pancakes at **Tryst** (p116) or the **Diner** (p116). On Sunday mornings the drag queen brunch at **Perry's** (p116) is the place to be.

☼ Stop in at the **District of Columbia Arts Center** (p115) and see what's showing in the gallery. Grab chopsticks next door for a rice bowl at **Donburi** (p115). Then spend the afternoon poking around the shops, such as **Meeps** (p119) for vintage wear or **Brass Knob** (p119) for salvaged building fixtures. Sate a sweet tooth at **CakeRoom** (p117) or hit happy hour at **Songbyrd Record Cafe & Music House** (p118).

☾ Hoo-wee, there's lots to choose from come nighttime. Have dinner at breezy **Tail Up Goat** (p115) or romantic **Mintwood Place** (p115). **Dan's Cafe** (p117) is a vintage, strong-pouring dive bar. For live music **Madam's Organ** (p118) puts on riotous blues and rock bands, while **Bukom Cafe** (p118) goes the reggae route. Fulfill late-night munchies at **Amsterdam Falafelshop** (p116).

♥ Best of Washington, DC

Eating
Tail Up Goat (p115)

Donburi (p115)

Diner (p116)

Shopping
Brass Knob (p119)

Idle Time Books (p119)

Meeps (p119)

Live Music
Madam's Organ (p118)

Bukom Cafe (p118)

Songbyrd Record Cafe & Music House (p118)

Getting There

Ⓜ **Metro** To reach most of 18th St, use the Woodley Park-Zoo/Adams Morgan station (Red Line). For points on 18th St south of Kalorama Rd, the Dupont Circle station (Red Line) is closer. Each station is about a 15-minute walk away.

🚌 **Bus** The DC Circulator runs from the Woodley Park-Zoo/Adams Morgan Metro to the corner of 18th and Calvert Sts.

15th St NW

Malcolm X Park

MERIDIAN HILL

W St NW

U St (0.3mi)

Florida Ave NW

16th St NW

16th St NW

Fuller St NW

Mozart Pl NW

Euclid St NW

Crescent Pl NW

Belmont St NW

Kalorama Rd NW

Florida Ave NW

V St NW

Seaton Pl NW

17th St NW

Ontario Rd NW

U St NW

Columbia Rd NW

Champlain St NW

California St NW

Lanier Pl NW

P 11
17

13 8
14 5
18th St NW 3
District of Columbia 1 Arts Center

6

10 15

18th St NW

12

16
KALORAMA

9

Dupont Circle (0.4mi)

Adams Mill Rd NW

2

7
4

Belmont Rd NW

ADAMS MORGAN

Kalorama Rd NW

Wyoming Ave NW

Mintwood Pl NW

Kalorama Park

Columbia Rd NW

19th St NW

Calvert St NW

Biltmore St NW

Waterside Dr NW

20th St NW

Kalorama Rd NW

Woodley Park (0.3mi)

200 m
0.1 miles

For reviews see	
Sights	p115
Eating	p115
Drinking	p117
Entertainment	p118
Shopping	p119

Sights

District of Columbia Arts Center

ARTS CENTER

1 Map p114, C2

The grassroots DCAC offers emerging artists a space to showcase their work. The 800-sq-ft gallery features rotating visual-arts exhibits, while plays, improv, avant-garde musicals and other theatrical productions take place in the 50-seat theater. The gallery is free and worth popping into to see what's showing. (DCAC; ☑202-462-7833; www.dcartscenter.org; 2438 18th St NW; admission free; ⊙2-7pm Wed-Sun; ⓜRed Line to Woodley Park-Zoo/Adams Morgan)

Eating

Tail Up Goat

MEDITERRANEAN $$

2 Map p114, C1

With its pale blue walls, light wood decor and lantern-like lights dangling overhead, Tail Up Goat wafts a warm, island-y vibe. The lamb ribs are the specialty – crispy and lusciously fatty, with grilled lemon, figs and spices. The house-made breads and spreads star on the menu too – say, flaxseed sourdough with beets. No wonder Michelin gave it a star. (☑202-986-9600; www.tailupgoat.com; 1827 Adams Mill Rd NW; mains $18-27; ⊙5:30-10pm Mon-Thu, 5-10pm Fri-Sun; ⓜRed Line to Woodley-Zoo/Adams Morgan)

Donburi

JAPANESE $

3 Map p114, C2

Hole-in-the-wall Donburi has 15 seats at a wooden counter where you get a front-row view of the slicing, dicing chefs. *Donburi* means 'bowl' in Japanese, and that's what arrives steaming hot and filled with, say, panko-coated shrimp atop rice and blended with the house's sweet-and-savory sauce. It's a simple, authentic meal. There's often a line, but it moves quickly. No reservations. (☑202-629-1047; www.facebook.com/donburidc; 2438 18th St NW; mains $10-15; ⊙11am-10pm; ⓜRed Line to Woodley Park-Zoo/Adams Morgan)

Mintwood Place

AMERICAN $$

4 Map p114, B2

In a neighborhood known for jumbo pizza slices and Jell-o shots, Mintwood Place is a romantic anomaly. Take a seat in a brown-leather booth or at a reclaimed-wood table under twinkling lights. Then sniff the French-American fusion dishes that emerge from the wood-burning oven. The *flammekueche* (onion and bacon tart), chicken-liver mousse and escargot hush puppies show how it's done. (☑202-234-6732; www.mintwoodplace.com; 1813 Columbia Rd NW; mains $18-30; ⊙5:30-10pm Tue-Thu, to 10:30pm Fri & Sat, to 9pm Sun, plus 10:30am-2:30pm Sat & Sun; ⓜRed Line to Woodley Park-Zoo/Adams Morgan)

Diner
AMERICAN $

5 Map p114, C2

The Diner serves hearty comfort food, any time of the day or night. It's ideal for wee-hour breakfast scarf-downs, weekend Bloody Mary brunches (if you don't mind crowds) or any time you want unfussy, well-prepared American fare. Omelets, fat pancakes, mac and cheese, grilled tofu tacos and burgers hit the tables with aplomb. It's a good spot for kids, too. (☑202-232-8800; www.dinerdc.com; 2453 18th St NW; mains $9-18; ☺24hr; ☝; Ⓜ Red Line to Woodley Park-Zoo/Adams Morgan)

Amsterdam Falafelshop
MIDDLE EASTERN $

6 Map p114, C2

Cheap and cheerful, fast and delicious, the Falafelshop rocks the world of vegetarians and those questing for late-night munchies. Bowl up to the counter, order your falafel sandwich, then take it to the topping bar and pile on pickles, tabbouleh, olives and 20 other items. Take away, or dribble away at the scattering of stools and tables. (☑202-234-1969; www.falafelshop.com; 2425 18th St NW; items $6-8; ☺11am-midnight Sun & Mon, to 2:30am Tue-Thu, to 4am Fri & Sat; ☝; Ⓜ Red Line to Woodley Park-Zoo/Adams Morgan)

Perry's
JAPANESE $$

7 Map p114, B2

You can munch sushi at Perry's, but it's the creative fusion fare that really deserves your tongue's attention. Eat in the attractive lounge or under the stars on the rooftop. Sunday brings something entirely different: drag-queen brunch. The megapopular campy show plus buffet is a scene to behold. Make reservations (up to two months in advance). (☑202-234-6218; www.perrysam.com; 1811 Columbia Rd NW; mains $15-26; ☺5:30-10pm Mon-Thu, 5:30-11pm Fri & Sat, 10am-3pm & 5:30-9pm Sun; Ⓜ Red Line to Woodley Park-Zoo/Adams Morgan)

Tryst
CAFE $

8 Map p114, C2

The couches, armchairs and bookshelves, and the light flooding through streetside windows, lure patrons so faithful they probably should pay rent at Tryst. They crowd in for the coffee, stellar omelet and waffle breakfasts, and creative sandwiches.

18th St, featuring the mural outside Madam's Organ (p118)

Come nightfall, baristas become bartenders, and the cafe hosts jazzy live music several nights a week. (☎202-232-5500; www.trystdc.com; 2459 18th St NW; breakfast & sandwiches $8-12; ⏰7am-midnight Sun-Thu, to 1am Fri & Sat; M Red Line to Woodley Park-Zoo/Adams Morgan)

CakeRoom   BAKERY $

 9 Map p114, C4

Ogle the glass cases bursting with creamy-frosted cakes and pies. The banoffee pie (a sublime banana-toffee mix) and date cupcake are the sweets to beat. Fadi, the baker, is from Jordan, and he invites guests to linger on the comfy couches and armchairs upstairs in the old-timey shop. (☎202-450-4462; www.cakeroombakery.com; 2006 18th St NW; baked goods $2.50-5; ⏰9am-9pm Mon-Thu, 9am-10pm Fri, 10am-10pm Sat, 10am-9pm Sun; M Red Line to Dupont Circle)

Drinking

Dan's Cafe   BAR

10 Map p114, C3

This is one of DC's great dive bars. The interior looks sort of like an evil Elks Club, all unironically old-school 'art,' cheap paneling and dim lights barely illuminating the unapologetic slumminess. It's famed for its whopping, mix-it-yourself drinks, where you get a ketchup-type squirt bottle of booze, a can of soda and bucket of

Top Tip

Late-Night Bites

Adams Morgan is famed for its late-night eateries. Lots of people come here post-party on weekend nights to soak up the booze. Huge slices of pizza are a traditional snack: they're sold everywhere around the neighborhood and are uniformly greasy and delicious after several libations.

ice for barely $20. Cash only. (☎202-265-0299; 2315 18th St NW; ⏱7pm-2am Tue-Thu, to 3am Fri & Sat; Ⓜ Red Line to Woodley Park-Zoo/Adams Morgan)

Songbyrd Record Cafe & Music House   CAFE

11 Map p114, C2

By day hang out in the retro cafe, drinking excellent coffee, munching delicious sandwiches and browsing the small selection of soul and indie LPs for sale. You can even cut your own record in the vintage recording booth ($15). By night the party moves to the bar, where beer and cocktails flow alongside burgers and tacos, and indie bands rock the basement club. (☎202-450-2917; www.songbyrddc.com; 2477 18th St NW; ⏱8am-2am Sun-Thu, to 3am Fri & Sat; Ⓜ Red Line to Woodley Park-Zoo/Adams Morgan)

Dr Clock's Nowhere Bar   BAR

12 Map p114, C3

The young and frisky seek out Dr Clock's for the offbeat decor – *Star*

Wars meets Soviet style – the cheap local beers and absinthe cocktails, and the solid DJs spinning weird techno and house music on Thursday, Friday and Saturday nights (no cover charge). The sign-less bar hides above the Rendezvous Lounge. (2nd fl, 2226 18th St NW; ⏱6pm-2am; Ⓜ Red Line to Woodley Park-Zoo/Adams Morgan)

Entertainment

Madam's Organ   LIVE MUSIC

13 ⭐ Map p114, C2

Playboy magazine once named Madam's Organ one of its favorite bars in America. The ramshackle place has been around forever, and its nightly blues, rock and bluegrass shows can be downright riot-inducing. There's a raunchy bar-dancing scene and funky decor with stuffed animals and bizarre paintings on the 1st floor. The rooftop deck is more mellow. The big-boobed mural outside is a classic. (☎202-667-5370; www.madamsorgan.com; 2461 18th St NW; admission $5-10; ⏱5pm-2am Sun-Thu, to 3am Fri & Sat; Ⓜ Red Line to Woodley Park-Zoo/Adams Morgan)

Bukom Cafe   LIVE MUSIC

14 ⭐ Map p114, C2

Killer reggae and highlife bands take the stage nightly at Bukom. Be prepared for sore but happy hips as you join the mix of West African immigrants and ex–Peace Corps types who've earned their dancing chops on the continent. The music starts at 10pm (earlier weekdays); there's no cover. Come early and sample the chicken yassa and other West African fare. (☎202-265-4600; www.bukomcafe.com; 2442 18th St NW; ☷4:30pm-2am; Ⓜ Red Line to Woodley Park-Zoo/Adams Morgan)

Shopping

Brass Knob
ANTIQUES

15 Map p114, C3

This unique two-floor shop sells 'rescues' from old buildings: fixtures, lamps, tiles, mantelpieces and mirrors. The store's raison d'être, though, is the doorknob – brass, wooden, glass, elaborate, polished and antique. If you need to accent your crib like the interior of the best old DC row houses, look no further. Staff can help you find whatever you need. (☎202-332-3370; www.thebrassknob.com; 2311 18th St NW; ☷10:30am-6pm Mon-Sat, noon-5pm Sun; Ⓜ Red Line to Woodley Park-Zoo/Adams Morgan)

Meeps
VINTAGE

16 Map p114, C4

There's this girl you know: extremely stylish and never seems to have a brand name on her body. Now, picture her wardrobe. Mod dresses, cowboy shirts, suede jackets, beaded purses, leather boots, Jackie O sunglasses and denim jumpsuits: there's Meeps mapped out for you. The store also carries a selection of clever, locally designed T-shirts. (☎202-265-6546; www.meepsdc.com; 2104 18th St NW; ☷noon-7pm Sun-Thu, to 8pm Fri & Sat; Ⓜ Red Line to Dupont Circle)

Idle Time Books
BOOKS

17 Map p114, C2

Three creaky floors are stuffed with secondhand literature and nonfiction, including one of the best secondhand political and history collections in the city. Its sci-fi, sports and humor sections are top-notch, and there's a good newsstand in its front window. (☎202-232-4774; www.idletimebooks.com; 2467 18th St NW; ☷11am-10pm; Ⓜ Red Line to Woodley Park-Zoo/Adams Morgan)

Local Life
Mixing it Up in Columbia Heights

Getting There

Ⓜ Green or Yellow Line to Columbia Heights, 3 miles north of the National Mall.

Columbia Heights booms with Latino immigrants and hipsters. A few decades ago the neighborhood was a tumbledown mess. Then the Metro station was built, followed by the slew of big-box retailers. And then – this is why you're here – it morphed into a cool-cat mix of ethnic eateries and unassuming corner taverns chock-full of local color.

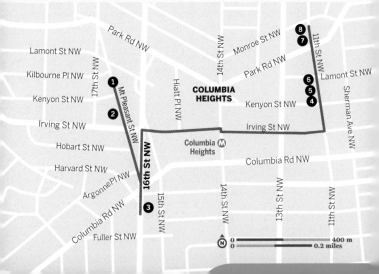

❶ Mt Pleasant Street

Mt Pleasant Street is the *corazón* (heart) of DC's Latino, largely Salvadoran community. Many businesses advertise money-transfer services to San Salvador or surrounds, or sell snacks from the homeland, or both. Take a stroll to see.

❷ Pupuseria San Miguel

Pupuseria San Miguel (☏202-387-5140; 3110 Mt Pleasant Ave NW; pupusas from $2; ⊙9am-10pm) is below street level and easy to miss. The humble little restaurant fries up delicious cheap *pupusas* (tortilla-like cornmeal pockets stuffed with cheese, beans or pork), a Salvadoran specialty and San Miguel's are renowned neighborhood-wide.

❸ Mexican Cultural Institute

The **Mexican Cultural Institute** (☏202-728-1628; www.instituteofmexicodc.org; 2829 16th St NW; admission free; ⊙10am-6pm Mon-Fri, noon-4pm Sat) looks imposing, but don't be deterred. The gilded beaux-arts mansion is open to the public and hosts excellent art and cultural exhibitions. You might see a show on Diego Rivera's art, Mayan religious artifacts or Octavio Paz's writings. Ring the doorbell for entry.

❹ Wonderland Ballroom

Divey **Wonderland Ballroom** (☏202-232-5263; www.thewonderlandballroom.com; 1101 Kenyon St NW; ⊙5pm-2am Mon-Thu, 4pm-3am Fri, 11am-3pm Sat, 10am-2am Sun) flaunts a spacious patio with outsized wooden benches that are just right on warm evenings. The upstairs dance floor sees a mix of DJs and bands, and gets packed on weekends. The interior is clapped out in vintage signs and found objects to the point where it could be a folk-art museum.

❺ BloomBars

BloomBars (☏202-567-7713; www.bloombars.com; 3222 11th St NW; by donation; ⊙hours vary) is a cool community arts center with children's story times and music classes by day, and gallery shows and world music concerts by night.

❻ Room 11

Room 11 (☏202-332-3234; www.room11dc.com; 3234 11th St NW; ⊙5pm-1am Mon-Thu, 5pm-2am Fri, 10am-2am Sat, 10am-1am Sun) isn't much bigger than an ambitious living room, and as such it can get pretty jammed. On the plus side, everyone is friendly, and there's a spacious outdoor area for when it gets too hot inside.

❼ Meridian Pint

Meridian Pint (☏202-588-1075; www.meridianpint.com; 3400 11th St NW; ⊙5pm-2am Mon-Thu, 5pm-3am Fri, 10am-3am Sat, 10am-2am Sun) is the quintessential corner tavern. Sports flicker on TV, folks play pool, and impressive American craft beers flow from the 24 taps.

❽ Maple

At snug **Maple** (☏202-588-7442; www.dc-maple.com; 3418 11th St NW; mains $16-23; ⊙5:30-11:30pm Mon-Thu, 5pm-1am Fri, 11:30am-1am Sat, 10:30am-11pm Sun), hot young residents eat pasta and sip housemade *limoncello,* on a reclaimed wood bar.

Top Sights
Arlington National Cemetery

Getting There

Ⓜ Blue Line to Arlington Cemetery, which is right by the entrance and visitors center. Though Arlington is in Virginia, it's only a few stops southwest of the National Mall.

Simple white headstones mark the sacrifice of over 400,000 service members and their dependents. The 624-acre grounds contain the dead of every war the US has fought since the Revolution. The cemetery is still in active use, and it's not uncommon to see families gathered around flag-draped caskets or hear a bugle's lingering notes of 'Taps' hang in the air.

Tomb of the Unknown Soldier

Tomb of the Unknowns

The Tomb of the Unknown Soldier contains the remains of unidentified US servicemen from both World Wars and the Korean War. A special military unit of white-gloved, rifle-toting sentinels maintains a round-the-clock vigil. The elaborate changing of the guard (every hour on the hour October through March, every half-hour April through September) is one of Arlington's most moving sights.

Kennedy Gravesites

An eternal flame marks the grave of John F Kennedy, next to those of Jacqueline Kennedy Onassis and their two children who died in infancy. Stones of Cape Cod granite pave the area; the clover and sedum growing in the crevices are meant to evoke a Massachusetts field. JFK's brother Bobby is buried 100ft southwest along the path. Youngest brother Ted also lies nearby.

Arlington House

Much of the cemetery was built on the grounds of **Arlington House** (📞703-235-1530; www.nps.gov/arho; admission free; 🕐9:30am-4:30pm), the former home of Robert E Lee and his wife Mary Anna Custis Lee, a descendant of Martha Washington. When Lee left to lead Virginia's army in the Civil War, Union troops confiscated the property to bury their dead. The home is open for tours.

Other Memorials

The Space Shuttle Challenger Memorial is near the Tomb of the Unknown Soldier. The USS Maine Memorial, marked by the battleship's huge mast, is also nearby. A bit further on is the controversial Confederate Memorial that honors war dead from the Civil War's breakaway states.

📞 877-907-8585

www.arlingtoncemetery.mil

admission free

🕐 8am-7pm Apr-Sep, to 5pm Oct-Mar

Ⓜ Blue Line to Arlington Cemetery

☑ Top Tips

▶ Pick up a free cemetery map at the visitors center.

▶ Hop-on, hop-off bus tours (adult/child $13.50/6.75) are an easy way to hit all the highlights. They depart continuously from the visitors center.

▶ If you have a smartphone, you can also download the excellent free ANC Explorer app.

✕ Take a Break

Ireland's Four Courts (📞703-525-3600; www.irelandsfourcourts.com; 2051 Wilson Blvd; 🕐11am-2am Mon-Fri, 8am-2am Sat & Sun; Ⓜ Courthouse) brings on the Guinness and shepherd's pie in classic pub style. It's 2 miles northwest of the cemetery.

The Best of
Washington, DC

Washington, DC's Best Walks

Iconic Washington 126
Embassies & Mansions 128

Washington, DC's Best...

Eating 130
Bars & Clubs 132
Shopping 133
Live Music 134
For Free 135
Museums & Monuments 136
For Kids 138
Gay & Lesbian 140
Theater & Performing Arts 141
Art & Architecture 142
History & Politics 143
Sports & Activities 144

The Capitol (p68)
ANDREA IZZOTTI/SHUTTERSTOCK ©

Best Walks
Iconic Washington

🏃 The Walk

This is a hit parade of DC's most celebrated sights. They huddle around the National Mall – 'America's front yard' – the 2-mile-long strip of grass between the Capitol and Lincoln Memorial. Iconic monuments dot the grounds to the west, hulking Smithsonian museums to the east, and at the northern edge the White House. Start early, especially in summer, to avoid the crowds and the heat.

Start Vietnam Veterans Memorial; 🚌 National Mall Circulator; Ⓜ Foggy Bottom-GWU

Finish White House; Ⓜ Federal Triangle or McPherson Sq

Length 3.75 miles; 2½ hours

🍴 Take a Break

Refuel at the Pavilion Cafe (p40), in the National Sculpture Garden.

❶ Vietnam Veterans Memorial

The Vietnam Veterans Memorial (p26) reflects a roll call of the war's 53,000-plus American casualties. Check the symbol beside each name. A diamond indicates 'killed, body recovered.' A plus sign indicates 'missing and unaccounted for.' There are approximately 1200 of the latter.

❷ Lincoln Memorial

Follow the masses to the Lincoln Memorial (p24). Commune with Abe in his chair, then head down the steps to the marker where Martin Luther King Jr gave his 'Dream' speech. From here, the view of the Reflecting Pool and Washington Monument is one of DC's best.

❸ Martin Luther King Jr Memorial

Mosey to the Tidal Basin; the Martin Luther King Jr Memorial (p36) stands by the water. Walk right around the towering statue and read the quotes on the walls.

KAMIRA/SHUTTERSTOCK ©

Lincoln Memorial (p24)

❹ Washington Monument

As you approach the Washington Monument (p28) look a third of the way up. See how it's slightly lighter in color at the bottom? Builders had to use different marble after the first source dried up.

❺ National Air & Space Museum

Simply step inside the Air & Space Museum (p30) and gaze up. Lindbergh's *Spirit of St Louis* and Chuck Yeager's sound-barrier breaking *Bell X-1* are among the history-making machines that hang from the ceiling.

❻ National Gallery of Art

Walk across the Mall to the neoclassical west building of the National Gallery of Art (p36). Ogle the Western Hemisphere's only Leonardo da Vinci painting in Gallery 6. The east building hangs works by Picasso, Matisse and other modern masters.

❼ National Archives

Enter the rotunda at the National Archives (p84). The Declaration of Independence, Constitution and Bill of Rights unfurl on parchment under glass.

❽ White House

Stroll up Pennsylvania Ave to E St NW and the White House (p44). Snap pictures across the South Lawn. Bonus points if you capture a helicopter landing on the grass.

Best Walks
Embessies & Mansions

🏃 The Walk

Embassies sprinkle the District, but Dupont Circle has the most. Massachusetts Ave was once Millionaire's Row, and the mansions of the old elite are still thick on the ground. Most embassies were residences built by industrialists and financiers at the turn of the 20th century. The Great Depression caused many to lose their manors, which stood gracefully decaying until WWII's end. As nations came to town to set up shop, the old homes were uniquely fit to be embassies.

Start Blaine Mansion; Ⓜ Dupont Circle

Finish Spanish Steps; Ⓜ Dupont Circle

Length 1 mile; 45 minutes

✕ Take a Break

Swill a brew from almost anywhere in the world at Bier Baron (p108), a half-block south of the Luxembourg Embassy.

Indonesian Embassy

BILL PERRY/SHUTTERSTOCK ©

❶ Blaine Mansion

In 1881 Republican party founder 'Slippery Jim' Blaine built the haunted-house-creepy Blaine Mansion at 2000 Massachusetts Ave, now the oldest mansion in Dupont. He lived there less than two years, not because he was spooked by bizarre architecture, but because his political fortunes changed.

❷ Indonesian Embassy

The Walsh-McLean-House at No 2020 is now the Indonesian Embassy. Gold-mining magnate Thomas Walsh commissioned the home in 1903. He embedded in the foundation a gold nugget, which has never been found.

❸ Anderson House

Continue up Massachusetts Ave to No 2118 and the grand Anderson House, base of the Society of the Cincinnati, a group that educates the public about the Revolutionary War. It's one of the few homes you can go inside. The ballrooms, chandeliers and staircases drop the jaw.

4 Luxembourg Embassy

The Luxembourg Embassy at No 2200 is a showstopper. Alexander Stewart built the home in 1909 in the grand court style of Louis XIV. In 1941 the Grand Duchess of Luxembourg bought it and lived there during WWII.

5 Sheridan Circle

Soon you'll approach Sheridan Circle, centered on Gutzon Borglum's equestrian statue of Civil War General Philip Sheridan.

Borglum later sculpted Mt Rushmore.

6 Turkish Ambassador's Residence

Edward Everett, inventor of the grooved bottle cap, built what is now the Turkish Ambassador's Residence, on the corner of Sheridan Circle and 23rd St. George Oakley Totten designed the building.

7 Croatian Embassy

At No 2343 Massachusetts Ave, a cross-legged

sculpture of St Jerome dreams over his book. The masterpiece is the work of Croatian sculptor Ivan Meštrović; appropriately, it fronts the Croatian Embassy.

8 Spanish Steps

Detour east on Decatur Pl to 22nd St. The rise up to S St NW was too steep, so city planners constructed a pedestrian staircase, dubbed the Spanish Steps for its resemblance to Rome's Piazza di Spagna. Climb up and stare across the area you've traversed.

Best **Eating**

AS FOOD STUDIO/SHUTTERSTOCK ©

A homegrown foodie revolution has transformed the once buttoned-up DC dining scene. Driving it is the bounty of farms at the city's doorstep, along with the booming local economy and influx of worldly younger residents. Small, independent, local-chef-helmed spots now lead the way. And they're doing such a fine job that Michelin deemed the city worthy of its stars.

Global Influence

Washington, DC, is one of the most diverse, international cities of its size in America, heavily populated by immigrants, expats and diplomats from every country in the world. People from far away crave the food of home, and so there's a glut of good ethnic eating and international influences around town. Salvadoran, Ethiopian, Vietnamese, French, Spanish, West African – they've all become Washingtonian.

Local Bounty

The city's unique geography puts it between two of the best food-production areas in America: Chesapeake Bay and the Virginia Piedmont. From the former come crabs, oysters and rockfish; the latter provides game, pork, wine and peanuts. Chefs take advantage of this delicious abundance.

Southern Influence

Keep in mind that DC also occupies the fault line between two of America's greatest culinary regions: the Northeast and the South. The South, in particular, exerts a tremendous pull. The city offers heaps of soul food and its high-class incarnations, so get ready to loosen the belt for plates of fried chicken, sweet-potato hash and butter-smothered grits – all washed down with sweet iced tea, of course.

Best for Foodies

Dabney Rustic room cooking up overlooked mid-Atlantic flavors. (p92)

Tail Up Goat Mediterranean shared plates in breezy, island-like environs. (p115)

Rose's Luxury Worth the wait for worldly comfort food and awesomely friendly service. (p73)

Best Budget

Donburi Fifteen seats at the counter for authentic Japanese rice bowls. (p115)

Simply Banh Mi Hidden cafe to gobble Vietnamese pho and lemongrass pork sandwiches. (p62)

THE WASHINGTON POST/GETTY IMAGES ©

Fiola Mare (p63)

Best Local Scene

Ben's Chili Bowl Gossip with locals while downing a half-smoke. (p111)

Bistrot du Coin Hearty French fare from steak *frites* to mussels. (p100)

Best Vegetarian

Chercher Veggie-rich Ethiopian stews in a colorful townhouse. (p93)

Shouk Bright-tiled eatery for vegan Israeli street food. (p94)

Best Seafood

Maine Avenue Fish Market Shrimp, crabs and oysters fried, broiled or steamed wharfside. (p78)

Fiola Mare Georgetown's sceney, river-view hot spot delivers the goods with an Italian twist. (p63)

Best Sweets

Baked & Wired This sunny cafe bakes DC's biggest, bestest cupcakes. (p59)

Un Je Ne Sais Quoi Vintage French pastries piled high with meringue and ganache. (p106)

Best Brunch

Ted's Bulletin Sink into a retro booth for beer biscuits and house-made pop tarts. (p78)

Diner Scarf omelets, berry pancakes and Bloody Marys 24/7. (p116)

Worth a Trip

Chowhounds hobnob at **Union Market** (www.union marketdc.com; 1309 5th St NE; mains $6-11; ⏱11am-8pm Tue-Fri, 8am-8pm Sat & Sun; Ⓜ Red Line to NoMa), a sunlit warehouse-turned-food-hall where culinary entrepreneurs sell their herbed goat cheeses and smoked meats. Among the stalls featuring prepared foods, everything from Burmese milkshakes to Korean tacos boggle taste buds. It's located a mile northeast of Union Station.

Best
Bars & Clubs

When Andrew Jackson swore the oath of office in 1800, the self-proclaimed populist dispensed with pomp and circumstance and, quite literally, threw a raging kegger. Folks got so gone they started looting art from the White House. The historical lesson: DC loves a drink, and these days it enjoys said tipples in many incarnations besides executive-mansion-trashing throwdowns.

MATT MUNRO/LONELY PLANET ©

☑ **Top Tip**

▶ Washington is a big happy-hour town. Practically all bars have some sort of drink and/or food special for a few hours between 4pm and 7pm.

Best Cocktails

Columbia Room Swirl exquisite drinks in the Punch Garden or Spirits Library. (p95)

Copycat Co Fizzy cocktails in welcoming, opium den environs. (p79)

Bar Charley Friendly Dupont spot that mixes the gingery Suffering Bastard in vintage glassware. (p107)

Best Beer

Bluejacket Brewery Genre-spanning suds made on-site, from sour blonds to barley wines. (p79)

Churchkey The hulking menu has 500 different beers, including 50 craft brews on tap. (p96)

Best Clubs

U Street Music Hall Casual, DJ-owned spot to get your dance on. (p111)

18th Street Lounge Sexy young things groove in a Dupont mansion. (p107)

Best Dives

Dan's Cafe It's like an evil Elks Club, with massive pours of booze. (p117)

Tune Inn Ah, beer swilled under mounted deer heads. (p72)

Best Local Scene

Right Proper Brewing Co House-made ales flow in Duke Ellington's old pool hall. (p111)

Wonderland Ballroom Edgy, eccentric, with oddball folk art and outdoor picnic tables for mingling. (p121)

Board Room Knock back draft beers and crush your opponent at Battleship, Operation and other games. (p101)

Best
Shopping

Shopping in DC means many things, from browsing funky antique shops to perusing rare titles at secondhand booksellers. Temptations abound for lovers of vinyl, vintage wares, and one-of-a-kind jewelry, art, and handicrafts. And, of course, that Abe Lincoln pencil sharpener and Uncle Sam bobblehead you've been wanting await...

JASON COLSTON/GETTY IMAGES ©

Best Markets

Eastern Market Butcher, baker and blue-crab maker on weekdays, plus artisans and farmers on weekends. (p73; pictured above right)

Flea Market Weekend browser for cool art, furniture, clothing, global wares and bric-a-brac. (p73)

Best Antiques

Book Hill Galleries, interior design stores and antique shops all in a row in Georgetown. (p58)

Brass Knob Salvaged lamps, mirrors, mantelpieces and heaps of doorknobs from old buildings. (p119)

Best Books

Capitol Hill Books So many volumes; they're even for sale in the bathroom. (p73)

Second Story Books Antiquarian books and old sheet music, plus cheap sidewalk bins to rummage in. (p109)

Kramerbooks New books on the shelves, hearty food in the cafe, happening into the wee hours. (p101)

Idle Time Books Great political and history stacks among the three creaky floors of used tomes. (p119)

Best Souvenirs

White House Gifts Presidential golf balls, T-shirts, snow globes: a quintessential spot for goofy DC trinkets. (p54)

National Archives Peruse the Archives Shop for when you need a Declaration-inscribed ruler or John Adams stuffed toy. (p84)

Best Fashion

Meeps Cowboy shirts, Jackie O sunglasses and magnificent duds from past eras. (p119)

CityCenterDC Glittery boutiques galore fill this shopping oasis. (p97)

Best
Live Music

Washington's musical taste splits in several directions. Its jazz affair started in the early 20th century, when U St NW was known as Black Broadway for its slew of music theaters. Duke Ellington grew up in the neighborhood, and his influence lingers on. Blues, rock and global music also waft out of atmospheric local halls.

SIPTRAVELALODY/SHUTTERSTOCK ©

Neighborhood Hubs

Loads of clubs besides jazzy ones cluster around U St between 7th St and 14th St NW. The bands vary – alt-rock, hip-hop, soul, funk, Caribbean – but the common thread is that the venues are intimate, with something indie-cool going on. Other areas to scope out are H St NE in Capitol Hill for hip rock clubs, and 18th St NW in Adams Morgan for raucous music houses and world beats.

Best Rock, Funk & Blues

Rock & Roll Hotel There's thrashing rock but also hip-hop, punk and metal in this down-and-dirty club. (p81)

Hamilton Alt-rock and funk bands plug in a stone's throw from the White House. (p54)

Madam's Organ Prepare for yee-hawin' wild times in Adams Morgan's bluesy hot spot. (p118)

Bukom Cafe Join the West African crowd getting their groove on to reggae beats. (p118)

Songbyrd Record Cafe & Music House Make your own record upstairs, then hear indie bands in the basement. (p118)

☑ Top Tip

▶ See the alt-weekly *Washington City Paper* (www.washingtoncitypaper.com) for comprehensive listings.

Best Jazz

Blues Alley The sophisticated icon has been bringing in top names since Dizzy Gillespie's day. (p65)

Jazz in the Garden Tune in amid whimsical artworks in the National Sculpture Garden. (p41)

Howard Theatre Historic venue where Ella Fitzgerald once sang, now home to big-name touring acts. (p111)

Best
For Free

Washington, DC, has a mind-blowing array of freebies. From the Smithsonian Institution's multiple museums, to gratis theater and concerts, to jaunts through the White House and Capitol, you can be entertained for weeks without spending a dime.

NICOLE S GLASS/SHUTTERSTOCK ©

Museum Mania

The Smithsonian Institution has an incredible bounty of free museums. Other gratis collections include the National Gallery of Art and United States Holocaust Memorial Museum. Plus all of DC's monuments are free to visit. See Best Museums & Monuments (p136) for more information.

Best Free Non-Museum Sights

National Archives Gape at the Declaration of Independence, Constitution and Bill of Rights. (p84)

Library of Congress The world's largest library displays centuries-old maps, bibles and Thomas Jefferson's books (p76)

Best Free Tours

White House Peek into the rooms of the President's abode. (p44)

Capitol Guides lead you through the white-domed sanctum of Congress, cluttered with statues and frescoes. (p68)

Ford's Theatre Explore the venue where John Wilkes Booth shot Abraham Lincoln. (p90; pictured above right)

Bureau of Engraving & Printing Watch millions of dollars get printed, cut and inspected. (p77)

National Public Radio Wave to your favorite correspondents as you walk past the newsroom. (p77)

Best Free Entertainment

Kennedy Center The Millennium Stage hosts a free music or dance performance daily at 6pm. (p54)

Shakespeare Theatre Company Each August the troupe puts on a Bard classic gratis. (p96)

Best Free Days at Paid Museums

Phillips Collection Free Tuesday through Friday for the permanent galleries. (p104)

National Museum of Women in the Arts Free the first Sunday the month. (p92)

Best
Museums & Monuments

There's nothing quite like the Smithsonian Institution, a collection of 19 artifact-stuffed museums, many lined up in a row along the Mall. Rockets, dinosaurs, Warhol paintings – even the 45-carat Hope Diamond lights up a room. Washington's monuments – potent symbols of the nation's history and its makers – add to the stockpile.

Smithsonian Stash

Thanks, James Smithson, you eccentric antimonarchist Englishman. That $508,318 gift you willed to the USA back in 1829 to create a 'diffusion of knowledge' paid off. The Smithsonian holds approximately 156 million artworks, scientific specimens and artifacts in its trove of museums. In accordance with Mr Smithson's wishes they're all free.

Other Museums & Exhibits

DC has many more museums beyond the Smithsonian. Freebies include the National Gallery of Art and United States Holocaust Memorial Museum. The National Archives and Library of Congress aren't technically museums, but they hold museum-caliber exhibits. Then there are a handful of admission-charging entities such as the impressive Newseum featuring an antenna from the World Trade Center (p90; pictured above left).

Monument Madness

Monuments are so prevalent you'd think it'd be easy to get one built. Not so. First you need Congressional approval. Then you have to raise a *lot* of money and agree on a design. Take the Martin Luther King Jr Memorial. The idea had been floating around for decades. Congress approved it in 1996; $120 million and 15 years later, it finally opened in August 2011.

☑ **Top Tips**

▶ Most monuments are open 24/7 and are particularly atmospheric to visit in the quiet of morning or lit up at night.

▶ Timed-entry tickets are needed for the Washington Monument, United States Holocaust Memorial Museum and National Museum of African American History and Culture. They do run out, so arrive early or preorder online (a small fee is required in some instances).

National Museum of African American History and Culture (p36)

Best Science Museums

National Air and Space Museum Rockets, missiles and the Wright Brothers' biplane. (p30)

National Museum of Natural History Gems, minerals, mummies and a giant squid. (p37)

Best History Museums

United States Holocaust Memorial Museum Brutal and impassioned exhibits about the millions murdered by the Nazis. (p70)

National Museum of African American History and Culture A powerful collection with Harriet Tubman's hymnal, Emmett Till's casket and more. (p36)

National Museum of American History

Everything from a piece of Plymouth Rock to Dorothy's ruby slippers. (p37)

Newseum The Unabomber's cabin and other artifacts from headline stories. (p90)

Best Art Museums

Reynolds Center for American Art & Portraiture Portraits on one side, O'Keeffe, Hopper and more on the other. (p86)

National Gallery of Art It takes two massive buildings to hold all the paintings and sculptures. (p36)

Phillips Collection Modern art in a house that puts you face-to-face with Renoirs and Rothkos. (p104)

Best Monuments

Lincoln Memorial Abe gazes across the Mall from his Doric-columned temple. (p24)

Vietnam Veterans Memorial The black wall reflects the names of the Vietnam War's 58,300-plus casualties. (p26)

Martin Luther King Jr Memorial Dr King's 30ft-tall likeness emerges from a mountain of granite. (p36)

Washington Monument The iconic obelisk, DC's tallest structure, offers unparalleled views from the top. (p28)

Best
For Kids

Washington bursts with kid-friendly attractions. Not only does it hold the nation's best collection of dinosaur bones, rockets and one-of-a-kind historical artifacts, but just about everything is free. Another bonus: green space surrounds all the sights, so young ones can burn off energy to their hearts' content.

KAMIRA/SHUTTERSTOCK ©

Advance Reservations

Some sights – including the International Spy Museum, National Archives, Washington Monument, Ford's Theatre and the Capitol – allow you to make advance reservations for a small fee. During peak season (late March through August), it pays to go online and do so up to a month prior if you want to avoid lengthy queues.

Rainy-Day Options

The Smithsonian has two Imax theaters on the Mall: one in the National Museum of Natural History, and the other in the National Air and Space Museum. The latter also holds the Einstein Planetarium. Schedules are amalgamated at www.si.edu/imax.

Films to Set the Mood

In *Night at the Museum 2: Battle of the Smithsonian* (2009), museum exhibits come to life for Ben Stiller in the National Air and Space Museum and National Gallery of Art. (FYI, the first film was set in New York City's American Museum of Natural History, and the third film takes place at London's British Museum.) In *National Treasure* (2004) Nicolas Cage finds a coded map on the back of the Declaration of Independence that leads to – that's right – national treasure! The sequel came out in 2007, and the third installment is supposedly in the works.

☑ Top Tips

▶ Most museums provide family guide booklets with activities kids can do on site; ask at the information desk.

▶ DC Cool Kids (www.washington.org/dc-cool-kids) features activity guides, insider tips from local youngsters on things to do, and museum info.

Best Museums

National Museum of Natural History The mummified kitty, tarantula feedings generate big squeals. (p37)

National Air and Space Museum Touch moon rocks and walk through space capsules. (p30)

National Air and Space Museum (p30)

National Museum of American History Gawp at the Star-Spangled Banner flag, and George Washington's sword. (p37)

Newseum Junior journalists report 'live from the White House' via the TV studio. (p90)

Best Entertainment

National Theatre Free Saturday morning performances, from puppet shows to tap dancers. (p97)

Discovery Theater The Smithsonian's kids' theater features cultural plays and storytelling. (p41)

Georgetown Waterfront Park Splash in the fountains and curlicue through the maze. (p59)

Best Kids' Cuisine

Diner Drawing materials for kids, booze for parents, 24-hour service and American food classics for all. (p116)

Ted's Bulletin Retro spot serving smiley-face pancakes and peanut-butter-and-jelly sandwiches. (p78)

Best Shops

International Spy Museum Everything from mustache disguises to voice-changing gadgets. (p90)

Tugooh Toys Wood blocks, ecofriendly stuffed animals and educational games line the shelves. (p65)

Worth a Trip

The **National Zoo** (📞202-633-4888; www.nationalzoo.si.edu; 3001 Connecticut Ave NW; admission free; ⏰9am-6pm mid-Mar–Sep, to 4pm Oct–mid-Mar, grounds 8am-7pm mid-Mar–Sep, to 5pm Oct–mid-Mar; Ⓜ Red Line to Cleveland Park or Woodley Park-Zoo/Adams Morgan) is the top banana of family sights in DC. Giant pandas, orangutans and lions roam against a lovely backdrop. Tip: the walk is downhill from the Cleveland Park Metro stop.

RITU MANOJ JETHANI/SHUTTERSTOCK ©

Best
Gay & Lesbian

ALEXANDER H. SCHULZ/GETTY IMAGES ©

DC is one of the most gay-friendly cities in the US. It has an admirable track record of progressivism and a fair bit of scene to boot. The rainbow stereotype here consists of well-dressed professionals and activists working in politics on LGBT issues such as gay marriage (legal in DC since 2010).

Neighborhood Hubs

The gay community concentrates in Dupont Circle, which sees a lot of action in its bars and cafes. In recent years the party has spread toward Logan Circle, a short distance east, where many gays live. U Street, Shaw and Capitol Hill also have active scenes and gay-friendly businesses.

Events

The big event on the calendar is Capital Pride (www.capitalpride.org) from early to mid-June. Some 250,000 people attend the party. The parade travels from Dupont Circle to Logan Circle. There's also DC Black Pride (www.dcblackpride.org) in late May, the nation's largest black pride festival.

Best for Fun

JR's Dupont pub where a young, well-dressed crowd kicks back and sings show tunes. (p101)

Larry's Lounge Neighborhood tavern that's perfect for people watching and stiff drinks. (p107)

Cobalt Venerable gay club with wild dance parties throughout the week. (p108)

Perry's The restaurant's drag-queen brunch packs the place every Sunday. (p116)

Dacha Beer Garden The freewheeling outdoor spot becomes an unofficial gay hangout on Sundays. (p95)

Kramerbooks Bookstore and bistro that's open late night for heavy flirting. (p101)

☑ Top Tips

▶ *Washington Blade* (www.washington blade.com) is a free weekly gay newspaper that covers politics and has lots of business and nightlife listings.

▶ *Metro Weekly* (www.metroweekly. com) is the rival weekly publication aimed at a younger demographic.

Best
Theater &
Performing Arts

Washington stages more than political theater. From the evening-wear elegance of the Kennedy Center to scrappy theater troupes in pubs, the nation's capital has an envious slate of performances. It caters to Shakespeare, classical-music and poetry-slam fans particularly well.

ANTON_IVANOV/SHUTTERSTOCK ©

Best Theater

Shakespeare Theatre Company The nation's top troupe does the Bard proud. (p96)

Woolly Mammoth Theatre Company Experimental theater that puts on edgy original works. (p96)

Studio Theatre Award-winning venue for contemporary plays, known for its powerhouse premieres. (p97)

Ford's Theatre Lincoln's assassination site is still an active playhouse, often staging works related to Abe. (p90)

Best Performing Arts

Kennedy Center DC's performing-arts king of the hill, home to the symphony, opera and more. (p54; pictured above right)

Busboys & Poets Nerve center for open-mic poetry readings and story slams. (p111)

Military Bands The Marine Corps, Air Force, Army and Navy make patriotic music at the Capitol. (p69)

National Theatre DC's glitzy grande dame hosts Broadway shows and big touring productions. (p97)

Best Comedy

Capitol Steps They take corny jabs at Congress in musical sketches à la 'Fiscal Shades of Gray.' (p96)

DC Improv National stand-up comics yuck it up alongside local amateurs. (p108)

☑ **Top Tips**

▶ Destination DC (www.washington.org/calendar) and Culture Capital (www.culturecapital.com) are good resources for event listings.

▶ Gold Star (www.goldstar.com/washington-dc) is a national ticket broker that sells discounted tickets (up to 50% off) to local performances.

Best
Art & Architecture

The National Gallery of Art and Reynolds Center for American Art & Portraiture are the big players, but Washington's art scene extends well beyond them. Specialty collections fill several smaller museums, and a host of imaginative galleries make their home in the city. The neoclassical, Federal-style and modern buildings that rise up from DC's streets are artworks in their own right.

ANTON_IVANOV/SHUTTERSTOCK ©

Best Galleries

District of Columbia Arts Center The grassroots group shows thought-provoking emerging artists in its humble space. (p115)

Touchstone Gallery Run by a group of 45 artists, Touchstone puts on vibrant contemporary exhibitions. (p92)

Dupont Underground Groovy exhibitions held in an abandoned streetcar station beneath Dupont Circle. (p101)

Best Underappreciated Museums

Textile Museum The nation's only collection of its kind, with galleries of splendid fabrics and carpets. (p50)

National Building Museum Exhibits on DC's architecture set in a dramatic, Corinthian-columned hall. (p92)

National Museum of Women in the Arts Works by Kahlo, O'Keeffe and 700 other female artists. (p92)

Best Modern Architecture

National Museum of the American Indian The curving limestone exterior blobs like an art-house amoeba. (p39)

National Gallery of Art IM Pei designed the angular, light-drenched east building. (p36)

Reynolds Center for American Art & Portraiture The courtyard's glass canopy drops the jaw. (p86)

 Top Tips

▶ Federal-style architecture was popular from around 1780 to 1830. It evoked the elegance of classical architecture overlaid with an emphasis on modesty and understatement – a style that represented America's evolving national identity.

▶ The best places at which to see it are Georgetown and Capitol Hill, where Federal-style row houses still line the streets.

Best
History & Politics

The president, Congress and the Supreme Court, the three pillars of US government, are here. In their orbit float the State Department, World Bank and embassies from around the globe. If you hadn't got the idea, *power* is why Washington exerts such a palpable buzz. There's a thrill in seeing all the history and politics up close.

Best Politico Bars

Off the Record Where Very Important People drink martinis, steps from the White House. (p53)

Round Robin Since 1850 bigwigs and lobbyists have swirled drinks and cut deals in the gilded bar. (p53)

Best Politico Restaurants

Le Diplomate DC's political glitterati flock here for a Parisian-style night out. (p94)

Old Ebbitt Grill Play spot the senator while cracking open an oyster. (p52)

Cafe Milano Famed place to twirl spaghetti and spy big shots in Georgetown. (p64)

Best for Seeing Politics in Action

Capitol Sit in on committee hearings to see how bills start winding their way toward becoming laws. (p68)

White House The protester-fueled political theater outside the building shows democracy at its finest. (p44)

Best Sites for History Buffs

Ford's Theatre View the box seat where President Lincoln was assassinated. (p90)

National Archives Ogle the Declaration of Independence on parchment under glass. (p84)

Lincoln Memorial Steps Stand where Martin Luther King Jr gave his 'I Have a Dream' speech. (p24)

Watergate Complex Check out the building synonymous with political scandal, thanks to Richard Nixon and his wiretaps. (p50; pictured above right)

Best
Sports &
Activities

The nation's capital comes together in ways unexpected and touching when sports are at stake. It's about the only thing that gets citizens as pumped as politics, and it's more accessible, if not quite as cutthroat. But residents don't just watch sports –they get active, too. Miles of trails crisscross the city, offering sweet hiking and cycling opportunities.

ANDRIY BLOKHIN/SHUTTERSTOCK ©

☑ Top Tip

▶ For all spectator sports, buy tickets direct from the team's website or stadium box office, or via StubHub (www. stubhub.com).

Best Spectator Sports

Nationals Park Cheap baseball tickets, the Racing Presidents, and hip eats and drinks make a fun evening. (p81)

Verizon Center The Capitals fight hard at hockey, and the Wizards shoot some mean hoops here. (p97)

Best Walking & Running

Mall Nothing inspires a run like this big green lawn studded with monuments. (p22)

C&O Canal Towpath Bucolic trail a few steps from Georgetown's shopping frenzy. (p61)

Georgetown Waterfront Park Riverside path to watch yachts and take a break at outdoor cafes. (p59)

Dumbarton Oaks Park Escape the crowds on wooded, bridge-crossed trails. (p62)

Yards Park Amble the boardwalk along the Anacostia River. (p73)

Best Guided Jaunts

Key Bridge Boathouse Paddle by monuments on twilight kayaking tours. (p61)

Bike & Roll Nighttime cycling rides around the illuminated Mall. (p149)

Best Cycling

Big Wheel Bikes Convenient rental shop near three ace cycling trails. (p149)

Capital Bikeshare Stations around the city rent two-wheelers for quick trips. (p149)

Survival Guide

Before You Go   146

When to Go 146
Book Your Stay 146

Arriving in Washington, DC   147

From Ronald Reagan
Washington National Airport 147
From Washington Dulles
International Airport 148
From Union Station 148

Getting Around   148

Metro 148
Bus 148
Taxi & Ride Share 149
Bicycle 149
Car & Motorcycle 149

Essential Information   150

Business Hours 150
Electricity 150
Money 150
Public Holidays 151
Telephone 151
Tourist Information 151
Travelers with Disabilities. 151
Visas. 152

Survival Guide

Before You Go

When to Go

Washington DC

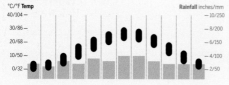

°C/°F Temp
Rainfall inches/mm

➡ **Winter (Dec–Feb)**
December is festive.
January booms if it's
an inauguration year.
Otherwise, low season
bargains abound. Gray
and chilly.

➡ **Spring (Mar–May)**
Peak tourism season
thanks to cherry blos-
soms and school-group
visits. Comfy weather.

➡ **Summer (Jun–Aug)**
Busy with summer
holiday crowds, lots
of festivals. Hot,
humid, 90-degree-plus
temperatures.

➡ **Autumn (Sep–Nov)**
Fewer tourists but
business travelers keep
hotel rates high. Cooler
weather; trees burst with
color.

Book Your Stay

➡ The White House area,
downtown and Dupont Cir-
cle are the most lodging-
filled neighborhoods.

➡ Washington's 14.5%
hotel tax is not included
in most quoted rates.

➡ For parking costs, figure
on $35 to $55 per day for
in-and-out privileges.

Useful Websites

➡ **Lonely Planet**
(www.lonelyplanet.com/
usa/washington-dc/ho
tels) Recommendations
and booking.

➡ **Bed & Breakfast DC**
(www.bedandbreakfast
dc.com) One-stop
shop to book B&Bs and
apartments.

➡ **WDCA Hotels** (www.
wdcahotels.com)
Discounter that sorts by
neighborhood, price or
ecofriendliness.

➡ **Destination DC** (www.
washington.org) Options

from the tourism office's jam-packed website.

Best Budget

Adam's Inn (www.adamsinn.com) Twenty-seven rooms to make yourself at home, in a couple of Adams Morgan townhouses.

Hostelling International – Washington DC (www.hiwashingtondc.org) Big, amenity-laden hostel that draws a laid-back international crowd.

William Penn House (www.williampennhouse.org) Quaker-run guesthouse with garden and dorms.

HighRoad Hostel (www.highroadhostels.com) Modern dorms and upscale amenities near Adams Morgan's nightlife.

Best Midrange

Hotel Lombardy (www.hotellombardy.com) International types tuck into handsome, antique-laden rooms.

Tabard Inn (www.tabardinn.com) Offbeat, TV-less rooms set in cozy Victorian row houses.

Chester Arthur House (www.chesterarthurhouse.com) Logan Circle manor stuffed with chandeliers, oriental rugs and character.

Kimpton Carlyle (www.carlylehoteldc.com) Oft-overlooked, art-deco beauty sitting amid Dupont Circle's embassies.

Cambria Washington DC Convention Center (www.cambriadc.com) Shiny new ecofriendly building with vast rooms and near the Convention Center.

Best Top End

Hay-Adams Hotel (www.hayadams.com) Old-school luxury a stone's throw from the White House.

The Jefferson (www.jeffersondc.com) Luxurious, romantic, Parisian and often considered DC's top address.

Willard InterContinental Hotel (www.washington.intercontinental.com) When visiting heads of state come to town, they snooze in the Willard's gilded suites.

St Regis Washington (www.stregiswashingtondc.com) Built to look like an Italian grand palace, with rooms opulent enough for nobility.

Arriving in Washington, DC

From Ronald Reagan Washington National Airport

➔ **Metro** The airport has its own Metro station (www.wmata.com) on the Blue and Yellow Lines. Trains (around $2.60) depart every 10 minutes or so between 5am and midnight (to 3am Friday and Saturday); they reach the city center in 20 minutes.

➔ **Shuttle van** The Supershuttle (www.supershuttle.com) door-to-door shared van service goes downtown for $16. It takes 10 to 30 minutes and runs from 5:30am to 12:30am.

➔ **Taxi** Rides to the city center take 10 to 30 minutes (depending on traffic) and cost $15 to

$22. Taxis queue outside the baggage-claim area at each terminal.

From Washington Dulles International Airport

➤ **Bus & Metro** Washington Flyer's (www. washfly.com) Silver Line Express bus runs every 15 to 20 minutes from Dulles (main terminal, arrivals level door 4) to the Wiehle-Reston East Metro station between 6am and 10:40pm (from 7:45am weekends). Total time to DC's center is 60 to 75 minutes, total bus-Metro tickets cost around $11.

➤ **Bus** Metrobus 5A (www.wmata.com) runs every 30 to 40 minutes from Dulles to Rosslyn Metro (Blue, Orange and Silver Lines) and on to central DC (L'Enfant Plaza) between 5:50am (6:30am weekends) and 11:35pm. Total time to the center is around 60 minutes; total fare is $7.

➤ **Shuttle van** The Supershuttle (www. supershuttle.com) door-to-door shared van service goes downtown for $30. It takes 30 to 60 minutes and runs from 5:30am to 12:30am.

➤ **Taxi** Rides to the city center take 30 to 60 minutes (depending on traffic) and cost $62 to $73.

From Union Station

➤ **Metro** There's a Metro (Red Line) stop inside Union Station for easy onward transport. The station is a few stops northeast of downtown.

➤ **Taxi** Taxis queue outside the main entrance. A ride to downtown costs around $7, to Dupont Circle $10.

Getting Around

Metro

➤ DC's modern subway network is the Metrorail (www.wmata.com), commonly called Metro.

➤ Trains start running at 5am Monday through Friday (from 7am on weekends); the last service is around midnight Sunday through Thursday and 3am on Friday and Saturday.

➤ There are six color-coded lines: Red, Orange, Blue, Green, Yellow and Silver.

➤ Fare cards are called SmarTrip cards. Machines inside all stations sell them. The plastic, rechargeable card costs $10, with $8 of that stored for fares. You then add value as needed.

➤ Fares cost $1.85 to $6, depending on distance traveled and time of day. Fares increase slightly during morning and evening rush hour.

➤ Use the card to enter *and* exit station turnstiles. Upon exit, the turnstile deducts the fare and opens the gate. If the value of the card is insufficient, you need to use an 'Addfare' machine to add money.

Bus

➤ DC's public bus system has two main fleets: Circulator and Metrobus.

➤ DC Circulator (www. dccirculator.com) buses run along handy local routes, including Union Station to/from the Mall (looping by all major museums and memorials), Union Station to/from Georgetown (via

K St), Dupont Circle to/ from Georgetown (via M St), and the White House area to/from Adams Morgan (via 14th St).

➡ Circulator buses operate from roughly 7am to 9pm weekdays (midnight or so on weekends). Fare is $1.

➡ Metrobus (www. wmata.com) operates throughout the city and suburbs, typically from early morning until late evening. Fare is $2.

➡ Pay with exact change, or use a SmarTrip card for all buses.

Taxi & Ride Share

➡ Taxis queue at Union Station, the main hotels and sports venues, but it's not always easy to hail one on the street.

➡ Fares are meter-based. The meter starts at $3.25, and then it's $2.16 per mile thereafter.

➡ There's a $2 surcharge for telephone dispatches. Try DC Yellow Cab (🕿 202 -544-1212) if you need a pickup.

➡ Ride-hailing companies Uber (www.uber. com), Lyft (www.lyft.

Money-Saving Tips

➡ Make the most of DC's abundant free sights and entertainment (p135).

➡ Take advantage of happy hour, when bars have drink and/or food specials for a few hours between 4pm and 7pm.

➡ Unlimited-ride Metro day passes cost $14.50, available at any station.

com) and Via (www.ride withvia.com) are popular in the District. Locals say they save time and money compared to taxis.

Bicycle

➡ **Capital Bikeshare** (🕿 877-430-2453; www. capitalbikeshare.com; per 1/3 days $8/17) has 3700-plus bicycles scattered at 440-odd stations, including many that fringe the Mall.

➡ Kiosks issue passes (one day or three days) on the spot. Insert a credit card, get your ride code, then unlock a bike.

➡ The first 30 minutes are free; after that, rates rise fast if you don't dock the bike.

➡ There's also an option for a 'single trip' ($2), ie

a one-off ride of under 30 minutes.

➡ Bike rentals for longer rides (with accoutrements such as helmets and locks) start at $16 per two hours. Try Bike & Roll (p76) or Big Wheel Bikes (p61).

Car & Motorcycle

➡ Avoid driving in DC. Traffic is constant, and street parking is scarce.

➡ Parking garages in the city cost $15 to $35 per day.

➡ Clogged rush-hour streets in DC include the main access arteries from the suburbs: Massachusetts, Wisconsin, Connecticut and Georgia Aves NW, among others.

Essential Information

Business Hours

Typical opening times in Washington, DC, are as follows:

Bars

5pm to 1am or 2am weekdays, 3am on weekends

Museums

10am to 5:30pm

Nightclubs

9pm to 1am or 2am weekdays, 3am or 4am on weekends

Offices & Government Agencies

9am to 5pm Monday to Friday

Restaurants

Breakfast 7am or 8am to 11am; lunch 11am or 11:30am to 2:30pm; dinner 5pm or 6pm to 10pm Sunday to Thursday, to 11pm or midnight Friday and Saturday

Shops

10am to 7pm Monday to Saturday, noon to 6pm Sunday

Electricity

Type A
120V/60Hz

Type B
120V/60Hz

Money

ATMs

➡ ATMs are available 24/7 at banks, airports and convenience shops.

➡ Most ATMs link into worldwide networks (Plus, Cirrus, Exchange etc).

➡ ATMs typically charge a service fee of $3 or more per transaction.

Credit Cards

➡ Visa, MasterCard and American Express are widely accepted at hotels, restaurants, bars and shops.

Tipping

Tipping is not optional. Only withhold tips in cases of outrageously bad service.

➡ **Airport & hotel porters** $2 per bag, minimum per cart $5.

➡ **Bartenders** 15% per round, minimum per drink $1.

➡ **Housekeeping staff** $2 to $5 per night.

➡ **Restaurant servers** 15% to 20%, unless a gratuity is already charged on the bill.

➡ **Taxi drivers** 10% to 15%, rounded up to the next dollar.

➡ **Parking valets** $2 to $5 when you're handed back the keys.

Public Holidays

Banks, schools, offices and most shops close on these days:

New Year's Day
January 1

Martin Luther King Jr Day
Third Monday in January

Inauguration Day
January 20, every four years

Presidents' Day
Third Monday in February

Emancipation Day
April 16

Memorial Day
Last Monday in May

Independence Day
July 4

Labor Day
First Monday in September

Columbus Day
Second Monday in October

Veterans Day
November 11

Thanksgiving Day
Fourth Thursday in November

Christmas Day
December 25

Telephone

US country code ☏1

DC area code ☏202

Making international calls Dial ☏011 + country code + area code + local number.

Calling other US area codes or Canada Dial ☏1 + area code + seven-digit local number.

Calling within DC Dial the seven-digit local number. If for some reason it doesn't work, try adding ☏1 then the area code at the beginning.

Tourist Information

Destination DC (☏202-789-7000; www.washington.org) DC's official tourism site, with the mother lode of online information.

Smithsonian Visitor Center (Map p34; ☏20 2-663-1000; www.si.edu/visit; 1000 Jefferson Dr SW; ⊙8:30am-5:30pm; ☏; Ⓜ Orange, Silver, Blue Lines to Smithsonian) Located in the Castle, it is a great resource with a staffed information desk and everything you ever wanted to know about the museum programs.

Travelers with Disabilities

➡ Most museums and major sights are wheelchair accessible, as are most large hotels and restaurants.

➡ All Metro trains and buses are accessible to people in wheelchairs. All Metro stations have elevators, and guide dogs are allowed on trains and buses.

Dos & Don'ts

Smoking Don't smoke in restaurants or bars: DC is smoke free by law in those venues.

Dining People eat dinner early in Washington, often by 6pm.

On the Metro Stand to the right on the escalators; walk on the left.

Conversation It's OK to ask locals you've just met, 'What do you do for work?' Most people in DC have an intriguing job that they're happy to discuss.

➡ All DC transit companies offer travel discounts for disabled travelers.

➡ Hindrances to wheelchair users include buckled-brick sidewalks in the historic blocks of Georgetown and Capitol Hill, but sidewalks in most other parts of DC are in good shape.

➡ All Smithsonian museums have free wheelchair loans and can arrange special tours for hearing-impaired visitors. See www.si.edu/Visit/VisitorsWithDisabilities

for more. Download Lonely Planet's free Accessible Travel guide from http://lptravel.to/AccessibleTravel.

Visas

The Visa Waiver Program (VWP) allows nationals from some 36 countries (including most EU countries, Japan, Australia and New Zealand) to enter the US without a visa for up to 90 days.

VWP visitors require an e-passport (with electronic chip) and approval under the Electronic System For

Travel Authorization at least three days before arrival. There is a $14 fee for processing and authorization (payable online). Once approved, the registration is valid for two years.

Those who need a visa – ie anyone staying longer than 90 days, or from a non-VWP country – should apply at the US consulate in their home country.

Check with the US Department of State (www.state.gov/travel) for updates and details on entry requirements.

Behind the Scenes

Send Us Your Feedback

We love to hear from travelers – your comments help make our books better. We read every word, and we guarantee that your feedback goes straight to the authors. Visit **lonelyplanet.com/contact** to submit your updates and suggestions.

Note: We may edit, reproduce and incorporate your comments in Lonely Planet products such as guidebooks, websites and digital products, so let us know if you don't want your comments reproduced or your name acknowledged. For a copy of our privacy policy visit lonelyplanet.com/privacy.

Karla's Thanks

Deep appreciation to all of the locals who spilled the beans on their favorite places. Thanks most to Eric Markowitz, the world's best partner-for-life, who kindly indulges my Abe Lincoln fixation. You top my Best List.

Acknowledgments

Climate map data adapted from Peel MC, Finlayson BL & McMahon TA (2007) 'Updated World Map of the Köppen-Geiger Climate Classification', Hydrology and Earth System Sciences, 11, 1633–44.

Cover photograph: Martin Luther King Jr Memorial, Sean Pavone/Alamy ©

Contents photograph: Capitol, Danita Delimont/Getty Images ©

This Book

This 3rd edition of Lonely Planet's *Pocket Washington, DC* guidebook was researched and written by Karla Zimmerman. The previous two editions were written by Karla Zimmerman and Adam Karlin respectively. This guidebook was produced by the following:

Destination Editors
Lauren Keith, Trisha Ping

Product Editor
Rachel Rawling

Senior Cartographer
Alison Lyall

Cartographer
Julie Dodkins

Book Designer
Virginia Moreno

Assisting Editors
Andrea Dobbin, Victoria Harrison, Gabrielle Stefanos

Cover Researcher
Marika Mercer

Thanks to
Kate Chapman, Joel Cotterell, Henning Eifler, Kate James, Kate Mathews, Jenna Myers, Lyahna Spencer, Andrew Wilkinson, Tony Wheeler

Index

See also separate subindexes for:

❽ **Eating p156**

❽ **Drinking p157**

❽ **Entertainment p157**

❽ **Shopping p157**

A

accommodations 146-7
activities 144
Adams Morgan 112-19, **114**
 drinking 117-18
 entertainment 118-19
 food 115-17
 itineraries 113
 shopping 119
 sights 115
 transportation 113
Anderson House 128
architecture 142
area codes 151
Arlington National Cemetery 122-3
art galleries 137, 142
ATMs 150

B

bars 132, see also individual neighborhoods, Drinking subindex
bicycling 61, 76, 144, 149
Big Wheel Bikes 61
Bike & Roll – L'Enfant Plaza 76
Bill of Rights 85
Blaine Mansion 128

Sights p000
Map Pages **p000**

bookstores 133
Booth, John Wilkes 91
budgeting 16, 135, 149
Bureau of Engraving & Printing 77
bus travel 148-9
business hours 150

C

Capital Crescent Trail 61
Capitol 68-9
Capitol Hill 66-81, **74-75**
 drinking 79, 81
 entertainment 81
 food 78-9
 itineraries 67, 72-3, **72**
 sights 68-71, 76-7
 transportation 67
car travel 149
cell phones 16
children, travel with 138-9
Chinatown 90
climate 146
clubs 132, see also individual neighborhoods, Entertainment subindex
C&O Canal Towpath 61
Columbia Heights 120-1, **120**
comedy 141, see also Entertainment subindex

Constitution 85
costs 16, 135, 149
credit cards 150
Croatian Embassy 129
currency 16
cycling 61, 76, 144, 149

D

Daughters of the American Revolution 50
Declaration of Independence 85
disabilities, travelers with 151-2
District of Columbia Arts Center 115
Douglass, Frederick 80
Downtown, Penn Quarter & Logan Circle 82-97, **88-89**
 drinking 95-6
 entertainment 96-7
 food 92-5
 itineraries 83
 shopping 97
 sights 84-7, 90, 92
 transportation 83
drinking & nightlife 132, see also individual neighborhoods, Drinking subindex
driving 149
Dumbarton Oaks 61
Dumbarton Oaks Park 62

Dupont Circle 98-109, **102-3**
 drinking 107-8
 entertainment 108-9
 food 104-7
 itineraries 99, 100-1, **100**
 shopping 109
 sights 104
 transportation 99
 walks 128-9, **129**
Dupont Underground 101

E

electricity 16, 150
Ellipse 50
Embassy Row 104, 128-9
entertainment 134, 141, see also individual neighborhoods, Entertainment subindex
etiquette 151
Exorcist Stairs 62

F

fashion 133
Foggy Bottom, see White House area & Foggy Bottom
food 130-1, see also individual neighborhoods, Eating subindex

food trucks 52
Ford's Theatre 90
Foundry Gallery 111
Franklin Delano Roosevelt Memorial 40
free attractions 135
Freer-Sackler Museums of Asian Art 39

G
galleries 137, 142
gay travelers 140
Georgetown 56-65, **60**
drinking 65
entertainment 65
food 62-4
itineraries 57, 58-9, **58**
shopping 65
sights 61-2
transportation 57
Georgetown University 61-2
Georgetown Waterfront Park 59

H
highlights 8-11, 12-13
history 38, 51, 80, 91, 143
Hoban, James 45
holidays 151

I
Indonesian Embassy 128
International Spy Museum 90
itineraries 14-15, 126-9

J
jazz 110-11, 134
Jefferson Memorial 39

K
kayaking 61
Key Bridge Boathouse 61

L
language 16
lesbian travelers 140
Library of Congress 76
Lin, Maya 27
Lincoln, Abraham 25, 91
Lincoln Memorial 24-5
local life 12-13
Logan Circle, see Downtown, Penn Quarter & Logan Circle
Luxembourg Embassy 129

M
Magna Carta 85
Maine Avenue Fish Market 78
markets 133
Martin Luther King Jr Memorial 36
Metro 148
Mexican Cultural Institute 121
MLK Marker 25
mobile phones 16
money 16, 150-1
monuments 136-7
motorcycle travel 149
Mt Pleasant Street 121
museums 136-7, 142
music venues 134

N
National Air & Space Museum 30-2
National Archives 84-5
National Building Museum 92
National Gallery of Art 36-7
National Geographic Society Museum 104
National Mall 22-41, **34-35**, **127**
entertainment 41
food 40-1
itineraries 23
sights 24-32, 36-7, 39-40
transportation 23
walks 126-7, **127**
National Museum of African American History & Culture 36
National Museum of American History 37
National Museum of Natural History 37-9
National Museum of the American Indian 39
National Museum of Women in the Arts 92
National Postal Museum 76
National Public Radio 77
National Sculpture Garden 36
National WWII Memorial 39
National Zoo 139
Newseum 90

O
Old Stone House 62
opening hours 150

P
Penn Quarter, see Downtown, Penn Quarter & Logan Circle
performing arts 141, see also Entertainment subindex
Phillips Collection 104
politics 143
public holidays 151

R
Reflecting Pool 25
Renwick Gallery 50
Reynolds Center for American Art & Portraiture 86-7
Roosevelt, Franklin Delano 40

S
Shaw 110-11, **110**
shopping 133, see also individual neighborhoods, Shopping subindex
Smithson, James 33
Smithsonian Institution 33, 136
Spanish Steps 129
sports 144
Studio Gallery 104
subway 148
Supreme Court 76

T
taxis 149
telephone services 16, 151
Textile Museum 50
theater 141, see also Entertainment subindex
time 16
tipping 16, 150-1

top sights 12-13
Touchstone Gallery 92
tourist information 151
tours 46, 123
train travel 148
transportation 17, 147-8,
148-9
Tudor Place 62
**Turkish Ambassador's
Residence 129**

U
U Street 110-11, **110**
**United States
Holocaust
Memorial Museum
70-1**

V
vacations 151
**Vietnam Veterans
Memorial 26-7**
visas 16, 152

W
walks 126-9, 144
Washington, George
28, 51
**Washington
Monument 28-9**
Watergate Complex 50
weather 146
websites 16, 146-7
White House 44-7
White House area
& Foggy Bottom
42-55, **48-49**
drinking 53-4
entertainment 54
food 52-3
itineraries 43

Sights p000
Map Pages **p000**

shopping 54-5
sights 44-7, 50
transportation 43

Y
Yards Park 73

⊗ Eating

A
A Baked Joint 93
Ambar 73
Amsterdam
Falafelshop 116

B
Baked & Wired 59
Ben's Chili Bowl 111
Birch & Barley 96
Bistrot du Coin 100
Blue Duck Tavern 107
BreadLine 53
Bub & Pop's 105
Bul 116

C
Cafe Milano 64
CakeRoom 117
Cascade Cafe 40-1
Central Michel
Richard 93
Chercher 93-4
Chez Billy Sud 64

D
Dabney 92-3
Diner 116
Dolcezza 101
Donburi 115
Duke's Grocery 101
Dupont Circle
Market 106

E
El Sol 94
Ethiopic 78

F
Fiola Mare 63
Food Truck Fiesta 52
Founding Farmers 52

G
Good Stuff Eatery 79

H
Hank's Oyster Bar
106-7

I
Il Canale 63
Ireland's Four
Courts 123

J
Jimmy T's 69

L
Le Diplomate 94
Le Grenier 79
Little Serow 104-5

M
Maine Avenue
Fish Market 78
Maple 121
Marcel's 52-3
Martin's Tavern 59
Matchbox Pizza 95
Mintwood Place 115
Mitsitam Native
Foods Cafe 40

O
Obelisk 105-6
Old Ebbitt Grill 52

Oohh's & Aahh's 111

P
Patisserie Poupon 59
Pavilion Cafe 40
Perry's 116
Pie Sisters 64
Pineapple
& Pearls 78
Pupuseria
San Miguel 121

R
Rasika 94
Red Apron
Butchery 85
Room 11 121
Rose's Luxury 73

S
Seventh Hill Pizza 79
Shouk 94
Sichuan Pavilion 53
Simply Banh Mi 62-3
St Arnold's
Mussel Bar 106

T
Tail Up Goat 115
Ted's Bulletin 78
Toki Underground 78
Tryst 116-17

U
Un Je Ne Sais
Quoi 106
Union Market 131
Unum 64

W
Woodward Takeout
Food 52

Z

Zaytinya 95
Zorba's Cafe 106

🍸 Drinking

18th Street Lounge 107
Bar Charley 107
Bardo Brewing 81
Bier Baron 108
Bluejacket Brewery
    79-81
Board Room 101
Cafe Bonaparte 65
Ching Ching Cha 65
Churchkey 96
Cobalt 108
Columbia Room 95
Copycat Co 79
Dan's Cafe 117-18
Dacha Beer Garden 95
Decades 108
Dr Clock's Nowhere
    Bar 118

Filter 108
Firefly Bar 108
Grace Street Coffee 64
Granville Moore's 81
Hotel Hive 25
Larry's Lounge 107
Little Miss Whiskey's
    Golden Dollar 81
Meridian Pint 121
Off The Record 53
Right Proper
    Brewing Co 111
Round Robin 53-4
Songbyrd Record Cafe
    & Music House 118
Tabard Inn Bar 101
Tombs 59
Tune Inn 72

🎭 Entertainment

BloomBars 121
Blues Alley 65
Bukom Cafe 118-19
Busboys & Poets 111

Capitol Steps 96
DC Improv 108-9
Discovery Theater 41
Fridge, the 73
Hamilton 54
Howard Theatre 111
Jazz in the Garden 41
JR's 101
Kennedy Center 54
Lockheed Martin
    Imax Theater 32
Madam's Organ 118
Millennium Stage 54
National Theatre 97
Nationals Park 81
Rock & Roll Hotel 81
Shakespeare Theatre
    Company 96
Studio Theatre 97
U Street
    Music Hall 111
Verizon Center 97
Wonderland
    Ballroom 121

Woolly Mammoth
    Theatre
    Company 96

🛍 Shopping

Book Hill 58
Brass Knob 119
Capitol Hill Books 73
CityCenterDC 97
Dupont Circle
    Market 106
Eastern Market 73
Flea Market 73
Idle Time Books 119
Kramerbooks 101
Meeps 119
Oliver Dunn, Moss
    & Co 65
Second Story Book 109
Tabletop 109
Tugooh Toys 65
W Curtis Draper
    Tobacconist 55
White House Gifts 54-5